# HOW TO GET ACTION:
## Key to Successful Management

# HOW TO GET ACTION:
# Key to Successful Management

## A. G. Strickland

**Parker Publishing Company, Inc.**
**West Nyack, N.Y.**

**Library of Congress Cataloging in Publication Data**

Strickland, A       G
  How to get action.

  1. Management.  I.  Title.
HD31.S6966          658.4       75-19412
ISBN 0-13-407239-1

Printed in the United States of America

# HOW YOU CAN USE THIS BOOK
## TO GET ACTION

You can increase your effectiveness by mastering a few simple ideas that get action. The manager who fails does so not from lack of knowledge but from lack of action—a lack of the right kind of action at the right time. This book has but one purpose: To help you get *the right kind of action* at *the right time* and *be a more successful manager*.

What do I mean by "action," and how can you be sure it is the right kind? I mean pay-off action. In other words, if you were selling door-to-door, what particular action would be absolutely necessary to lead directly to a sale, with cash in hand? This is the ultimate test. Every man working in business or industry should have a breaking-in period when he has to knock on doors and sell to see just how much action is required to bring in a certain amount of money. Of course, since that isn't feasible, that's where you as a manager come in. You must know and be able to communicate to your men what pay-off is. By the time you finish this book you will think and act in terms of the right kind of action.

You've got to get people to do things. That means assigning work. Can you pick the right man? Or do you take the one who is the nearest, the one who isn't busy, or the one you like to deal with? If so, you may end up with one man overworked and another sitting around idle. You may create strong resentment because one man gets all of the assignments. As you read this book, you'll look at who you select and why and, in turn, pick up your batting average of getting the right man for the right job.

5

How well do you define and develop the assignment while giving it to that man? Why not learn the easy ways to break down each part of the job so that it can be checked to keep track of how well it is going?

You have probably set high standards for yourself already—that's why you made it into a leadership spot. These same standards must be transmitted to your people in such a way that they can be met. That's where many managers take a nosedive. If the manager keeps driving for performance when these standards aren't clearly defined and transmitted, he gets frustrated workers. He gets wheel-spinning. One chapter helps you define quality, time and costs. In addition, it deals with the "unknown" standards. These really make or break your men and yet usually get skipped over in definition. In addition, you'll learn to evaluate how well your men really understand your standards and instructions.

As an action-getting manager, you aren't satisfied with a response like "I told him." You're going to drive to see that work is done on time or else. That's where the chapters on checkpoints and feedback will be particularly helpful. Are there clear signs that your worker won't make it? What are the symptoms of things going wrong? You will learn how to recognize these—how to look at, listen to and feel what's going wrong, and to get back in the act in time to assure the results you want.

Your success is related to how well you handle people. You may be able to force people to do something this time, but how about the next time when you need action? One Sunday in church a youngster, three or four years old, sat with his mother on the seat ahead of me. He kept climbing up on the seat, looking over the back and making faces at me. His mother kept pulling him back down. Finally the last time she pulled him down, she looked sternly at him and whispered, "Now you sit down and stay down." He glared back at her and replied, "All right, but I'm still standing up inside." You may force someone to do something, but he may still be standing up inside. This book will improve your chances for success by showing you ways to persuade rather than force people to take action.

A person who performs well may deserve more than his monthly paycheck to tell him so. Perhaps you can give him a pat on the back occasionally, or let him represent you in a meeting, or let him help train a newcomer. These are just a few of the many ways that you can show an employee your appreciation for his good work. Learn how to use these and other suggestions so you can avoid being a Johnny-one-note manager who thinks pay alone is the goal. You can even give criticism so that it doesn't curl the fellow's hair. The difference between destructive and constructive criticism lies not in how you give it but how the other man receives it. You'll want to learn the many techniques for correction without explosion.

Are you one of those men in the management spotlight who says, "I can talk to one person, but don't put me in front of a group"? Does your group just suffer in silence? Now's your chance to learn how to brighten up your meetings. Chaper 11 deals entirely with capitalizing on your own abilities to run successful meetings: how to determine who will attend; ways to keep everyone awake and participating; controlling it; getting results after the meeting is over; and best of all, how to give your confidence a boost.

It's terribly easy to sit and philosophize eternally about good management. Somewhere along the line a person must stop thinking and speculating and start putting his plan into action. The test of a plan is how great it is when operating. You must be able to put thought in action. That is your goal if you are going to be a great manager. The goal of this book is to help you do it as easily and efficiently as possible.

*A. G. Strickland*

# CONTENTS

# 1

## HOW TO GET ACTION AND
## LEAD TO SUCCESS AS A MANAGER

A picture which appeared recently in a magazine showed a magnificent four-lane highway in Kansas zooming out across the prairie and ending in a wheat field. Many times our magnificent efforts, like this highway, culminate in nothing. The manager's report card shows results, not effort expended. How often have we listened to excuses, rationalizations, and hallucinations about what transpired along the way—and yet there were no results.

What are the factors involved in getting action rather than excuses? Why does one man get action when another doesn't? Let's ferret out a few simple principles of our everyday lives. People who get action most easily have already used these principles. They *think* action. They *expect* action. They *demand* action.

How does an average individual in business get results in dealing with people above him, below him, and across the line? There are no infallible concrete rules . . . certainly none that can be followed religiously to a guaranteed end. There are, however, examples that offer clues. In examining thousands of examples of failures and successes, certain *action-getting principles* rise to the surface. The moment a man learns and applies these, he's no longer an average individual in business. He's one of the chosen few who move along.

Let's study these, shall we?

## HERE'S WHAT ATTITUDE
## DOES TO ONE MAN

Perhaps I should apologize for starting with Sam Unger. Sam could be a relative of someone close to you. Maybe your company has an employee like him. Sam is the real McCoy.

Sam once sat in my office and told me for exactly one hour and ten minutes that he had too much work to do: his bosses should have realized this and yet they seemed to give him more. He had just been in a meeting where he had explained his failure to deliver the goods. As you might suspect, it was because he was swamped with work. After several ruses, I managed to pry Sam's tentacles loose from my desk and send him along his way. I felt relieved because I thought maybe he would dig into some of that oppressive load he had on his shoulders.

Unfortunately, he had to pass Mr. Young's office on his way back. One of his tentacles suction-cupped to Mr. Young's desk and he settled down for a long tête-à-tête on the problem of his work load. One hour and a half later he was still there complaining. I've since learned that's his standard pattern.

He is the man who talks and does not act.

The more he is assigned, the more he talks.

Would you like to determine the solution?

Should his boss, who has tried several approaches so far, hold him to a due date on each item assigned? Should he threaten? Should he discuss the problem man-to-man? It may be hard to pin down an exact management solution without knowing the individual personally, but it's easy to recognize a complete pattern or an attitude.

Until the attitude is changed, this man is lost from the action-getting fold.

Read on . . . we'll talk about attitudes.

Let's talk first about your *self-confidence, confidence in your idea or product,* and the *attitudes of the other person.*

## HOW TO STRETCH YOUR LEVEL
## OF CONFIDENCE AS A BASE FOR
## SUCCESSFUL MANAGEMENT

Your store of confidence has to supply many people. It not only keeps you operating, but transfuses everyone that works under you: you're the confidence bank. So you need a good base of confidence if you are going to be an action-getting manager. Let's start now to build it. You can learn from a telephone operator who wanted to be a salesman:

One lady, after 19 years of answering a switchboard, decided that she wanted to sell Yellow Page ads for the telephone company. But before she could start, she had to overcome a serious handicap. Though she found it easy to talk to people over the telephone, she froze up in face-to-face conversations. She entered a class to try to get rid of this habit. Her release for nervousness, when she first stood up to talk, was a silly giggle. By the fourth and fifth times that she was called on to speak, the giggle had become a hysterical sob, and the sixth time, she broke into a loud wail and rushed toward the back door—anything to escape the torture this situation provoked. The instructor stuck out one arm and caught her as she headed past and conducted the rest of the class with a weeping, wailing woman draped over one shoulder.

That was the turning point for this lady. It was then that she became painfully aware of her habits. All of her nervous fear was exposed, and she admitted it. She bolstered her courage and tried again. She changed her thinking about what she could and couldn't do.

The next week she came bouncing in to class full of excitement and enthusiasm. "I'm ready to try again," she said, "I couldn't possibly do anything worse than I did last week." She became a relaxed speaker, and eventually the most effective person selling Yellow Page ads for the telephone directory in her city.

If you are to be an expert in getting action from others, you must first bolster your own confidence. This involves knowing yourself (which requires self-honesty) and accepting yourself (which requires admitting, at least temporarily, your own faults and limitations).

## THE FIRST STEP IN IMPROVING: ADMIT A DEFICIENCY!

If you're really poor in detail work, admit it to yourself. If you're poor in following up, admit it to yourself—even laugh about it at the moment. Laugh now, improve later.

I once filled out a travel report incorrectly, since I am no good at certain kinds of details and I know it. When I turned in the travel report, my secretary chewed me out for making her type it twice because of the error. Now I'm not defending that error, because it was careless, but nevertheless I made it and am likely to make another on the same kind of report. I looked her in the eye and said, "Willa, you ought not to get mad about that. That is what you are here for: to keep me out of trouble. You are really good at catching that kind of mistake and that's part of your value to the company. We need people like you to keep people like me on the ball." She purred like a kitten, apologized for taking me to task, and has been anxious to help me with my reports ever since. It isn't always necessary to defend your own weaknesses. Admit them, and as in this case, make the most of them—but go on to improving yourself.

Confidence comes from knowing you can do a good job in spite of your faults, and not from thinking you don't have any.

## CUTTING YOUR WEAKNESS DOWN TO SIZE

Dave Swartz, author of *The Magic of Thinking Big*, pulled this trick in one of his famous lectures. He asked each member of his audience to look at the person on his left carefully. Then he said, "Remember two things: he's not one-half as smart as you think he is; secondly, he thinks you are twice as smart as you are." That's pretty good advice. It certainly puts opinions of ourselves and others in perspective.

It is easy to magnify your own faults and think that everyone else sees you the same. Self-consciousness or a feeling of inadequacy is like the hole in your sock. No one else knows it's there. It doesn't really show, if you'll forget it. Even if your toe is sticking through the hole and you can wiggle it, it still is hidden in your shoe and no one knows about it. Few people realize the insecurities in the bosoms of other men.

To paraphrase a line from Joshua Liebman's *Piece of Mind:* "If we could look inside the other person at scars from the battles he has lost, our own scars would weigh less heavy."

Doris Hayden is a portrait painter. She has painted some of the most important people in her city. One of her latest portraits was that of the vice president of a large bank, and she tried her hardest on it.

Everyone that saw the painting liked it—the bank officer, his friends, his co-workers—everyone except one person . . . his wife. This wasn't the first time that Doris had had a painting that the wife of a subject didn't like.

Doris pondered the variables and finally arrived at a conclusion that seemed to apply to situations in the past as well. She had painted the man in all his glory. He reigned in the office. His associates saw him that way; the picture showed him that way. However, his wife didn't spend time in the office but in the home. She saw him in his underwear! Doris credits the wife's dislike of the picture to her difference in perspective. She is the only one who sees her husband in his underwear! You see yourself in your underwear and know your weaknesses. You must be able to evaluate weaknesses in relation to strengths and cut them down to size.

## HOW TO REMOVE EXCUSES BY EXPECTING AND DEMANDING ACTION

One of the sharpest managers in the Wood Company is Roy Streeter. If you could follow him around for one day, his method of operation would teach you more about action-getting than a dozen books. He exudes the expectation of action. Let's look at some of his characteristics:

He makes clear-cut assignments with a date of expected results. When that day comes he checks to see that he got what he wanted. He has a follow-up system that enables him to check on each assignment at the right time. (You will read more about these techniques in Chapter 8.) He accepts no excuses, and can get rather nasty if his requirements are not met. In general, he runs a tight shop. He's a pretty good guy, though demanding. Good guys don't finish first unless they are ready to stick to their requirements like Roy does.

In a quality control meeting where problems that cut across many department lines were being aired, one of Roy's supervisors stated that the electrical wiring on a product needed a better system of checking and control. Another supervisor, who would end up doing the checking and buying the equipment, said he didn't agree. The suggestion was almost dropped, until the first supervisor got red in the face and restated it. Roy straightened up in his chair and said, "Mr. X, I want a report next Wednesday on the number of errors, recurrence, and cost and time needed to install the better system." He noticed the sincerity and urgency in the first supervisor's manner. It turned out this man was absolutely right and saved the company money in the long run. It would have been easy to drop the issue when the second supervisor disagreed, but Roy spotted the problem.

If Roy finds a man in a key spot who is weak on action-getting, but circumstances won't allow his removal, Roy will assign a second man that does know how to get action to back him up on a project. Roy's ideas are like crabgrass: they keep cropping up everywhere. He plants ideas for future action and lets them grow. Someone soon starts cultivating an idea and it blooms. You can emulate Roy by creating an attitude that expects and demands action and cuts down excuses.

## ENSURE THAT TROUBLE DOWN THE LINE ISN'T JUST MENTAL

First, examine the price you pay for a poor attitude.

The personnel manager at a bus body plant told this story about his production line. A man working on the line was doing poorly and was moved to another spot. An incident occurred that indicated he was doing poorly again. He fainted and fell to the floor. Someone rushed over and gave him artificial respiration. The workers moved him to a first aid station and called a doctor. The doctor examined him and said, "There's absolutely nothing wrong with him except hysteria." He was so afraid of failing that he literally thought himself into almost dying. A fear of trying something and failing can keep a man from using his best abilities. It's a built-in handicap. You must help your men remove any such hang-ups before they can do their best.

## HOW MENTAL HANG-UPS
## STOPPED SEVERAL MEN

A man I know stated that he missed a couple of good opportunities to go into business. Someone offered to sponsor him, but he passed it up because he was afraid he would fail. Consequently, he kept a second-rate or a third-rate job. He was secure from having to make action-getting decisions, will never develop his best abilities until something shakes that attitude loose.

If you are asked to walk a board placed on the floor, you could do it with ease—but if it were moved up between two buildings, you can bet your bottom dollar there wouldn't be one in ten who could walk it. In considering the challenge and looking at the height, the thought "I might fall, I might fall" would start picking away at the mind. Most of us would not attempt to make it across the board. The fear of failing would triumph. In management we must shut out a voice which says, "I might fail, I might fail."

A young man enrolled in a large university. He was an "A" student in high school and was destined to do well at the university—until he became concerned . . . overly concerned. He worried about making poor grades because he had heard that the school was hard. Sure enough, he almost flunked out. In fact, he ended up on a psychiatrist's couch trying to get at the root of his trouble. If you are to be an action-getter, you must start by removing any mental hang-ups about failing.

## GIVING SERVICE YOURSELF

I met a man in the hall on the way to lunch and said, "Dewitt, we need a couple of boxes of anniversary brochures delivered from the warehouse to Mr. Poindexter in Field Service." He said, "O.K., I'll take care of it."

Two days later, I asked him if he had delivered the boxes. He replied, "You better believe it! Didn't I tell you I would?" Wonder of wonders, he had. That's what I call service. His "You better believe it" indicated that he didn't know anything except giving service.

We talk about demanding service and expecting service, but the $64,000 question is: "Can you give service?"

Mary Leitz owns and manages a shop which is flourishing. She serves visitors, tourists, conventioneers and local people that want a little color. Mary sells every kind of item to take home to Mama, wrap for Christmas or just hang on the walls. She watches as kids pick up candles and rap them on the side of the case and break them, as little old ladies pick up the same item a hundred times, turn around, look at the bottom and then put it down, and as a semi-drunken celebrator asks for a package to be wrapped to take home to the wife. She lives and breathes in an atmosphere of customer service, and she is extremely successful.

I went to lunch with her the other day and we sat and waited twenty minutes for a waiter, then twenty more minutes for food. She literally seethed. Her comment is worth quoting: "Since I started serving the public and waiting on people, I have no tolerance for poor service. I expect the other person to give me the good service that I would give him." She knows how to give service and therefore really has earned the right to demand the same.

As a manager, be sure you know how to do things for other people as you promise and when you promise, before you expect others to do this for you. This is a vital part of your attitude.

## HOW TO GIVE YOURSELF A PEP TALK

Any successful manager knows how to give himself a pep talk. He might deny it if you ask him. If you mentioned it, he might not even know what a pep talk is. But if he's successful, he's learned how to use one. He knows how to infuse himself with a positive spirit or attitude which gives him the energy to do the same for others. He bolsters his own thinking and assurance in order to do the same for the people who work for him. A pep talk is telling yourself that you *can* do something or that it *can* be done. It consists of spoken or unspoken crystallized positive thoughts that feed into the brain.

A simple example is the remembering of names. If you ask almost anyone how well he remembers names, he'll say badly. Why? The reason is that we only remember the times we forgot a name. You see somone in the hall and say, "Hi . . . er, and ah . . . hello." When he leaves, you think, "What was his name?" and you are embarrassed. That etches itself in your mind and will stick with you. You meet Sam Jones coming down the hall and say, "Hi, Sam." Nothing impresses your mind: you take it for granted. So you remember the failures and not the successes. You begin to tell yourself: "Gosh, I can't remember names worth a hoot." The more you tell yourself that, the truer it becomes. You're a victim of a pep talk, but a different kind—a negative pep talk.

Another example is the old business of speaking. Nobody will say to you, "Am I a good speaker." Very few people will say they can even speak. Most folks will say, "I'm scared to death," "I shake," "I don't know what to say," or something similar. Each time you or I make a statement like that we make it more of a reality. We are giving ourselves negative pep talks.

A positive example is the case of whistling in the dark. While you're not talking, you're acting in a positive manner, and before long you build a little confidence.

Managing must be approached with positive manner, with confidence, if you are to get action. A positive pep talk can be the answer. Here is a good example of how this can be done:

> Frank D. is one of 20 or 25 managers in a warehousing and supplies company. After much encouraging from the government, the company decided to start a plan emphasizing equal opportunity for all employees. This included setting standards and adhering to them without discrimination. The majority of managers laughed at the plan and professed to be following it, but really put little effort into making it work. Consequently, it didn't work in their areas.
>
> It did work in Frank's department. One of the reasons was that Frank talked to himself before he talked to his people. He gave himself a positive pep talk, saying that the basic principles were sound, that it was going to take time, that the government and his top management wanted it, and that it was up to him to make it work.
>
> He spent four hours studying the material before he had the first meeting with his people. When he talked to them, it sounded like his idea

and his material. He got them to participate, avoiding all inference that they were being forced to do it. Frank's supervisor also rolled up his sleeves to make the plan work. In subsequent meetings they even came up with creative additions to the plan.

When you give yourself a pep talk on how you can make something work, you're on a better base for making it come true.

## STARTING WITH A BELIEF THAT THERE IS A WAY TO GET THE RESULTS YOU WANT

On Saturday the youngster from next door came over to get some information on Theater Guild. She borrowed the encyclopedia and, after looking it up, found only scant information and wanted more. Her brother suggested calling the Theater Guild downtown. She couldn't find it listed in the phone book, so she put it down and said, "No, that won't work." He said, "O.K., what about calling our local Theater Central. Surely they will know." And then she said, "Well, this is Saturday." He said, "So what?" She replied, "Everything's closed on Saturday." "Well, call and find out," he persisted. She still hemmed and hawed.

Finally, he took the phone book out of her hand and called the number of the office. Sure enough, it was closed. Then he called the number of the box office. It was open, and the attendant gave him the phone number of one of the officials of Theater Central, an authority who could be contacted for the information needed for the report.

None of this would have happened if they hadn't persisted. A manager is lost if he starts a project believing it can't be done. Not only is he less prepared, but also his men adopt his attitude.

Someone somewhere can always help you get what you want. It's just a matter of making connections. It might not be *that* easy, but your attitude will get you halfway there.

## WHY YOU MUST SELL YOURSELF ON THE ACTION BEFORE APPROACHING SOMEONE ELSE

Dick James sold a good brand of encyclopedias. He called at a home one day to make his first sale. The people were not very well off financially, yet Dick sold them a set. He left, drove around the block, and then drove back, walked in and told the lady of the house, "You don't need these books . . .," tore up the contract and walked out. He quit selling then and there, stating, "I can't sell things I don't believe in to people who don't need them." Well, *who can?*

Abe Lincoln wasn't rich. Suppose he had not had access to books. Who knows that these people shouldn't have their desires satisfied? Who can judge the relationship between mind and stomach?

The first step in selling an idea or product is to honestly believe in it yourself. The second is to believe it can do something for the potential customer, either physically or mentally. If a man or a product cannot qualify on these counts, then don't sell.

Suppose you're lukewarm and you just can't quite hack it. Go to work! The first answer lies in knowledge—either of product or customer. Learn all there is to know about your product or idea and what it can do for people. Why is it better than someone else's? Go to headquarters and get the whole story. Who makes it and how? In other words, know your product. Try to learn some of the generalities of selling such as "People buy what they want—not what they need," etc. Next, learn the individual that you are selling. What does he like, dislike, want and need? Then slowly and surely fit your product to him. If it doesn't fit, revise your approach until it does. Then let the customer know about it.

Joe Camish had the job as a manager in a manufacturing company of putting a quality motivation program into effect in his department. The company had decided it was needed, yet Joe couldn't believe in it. First he attended several high-level meetings to learn all about it; then he studied one organization where it was working; finally, he started working on his own men. His first step, though, was to get sold himself.

Sell yourself the idea first. Action begins with an attitude—an attitude of confidence in yourself, plus confidence in your product or idea. An idea isn't good on its own; only acceptance makes it so. A non-receptive attitude on the part of the recipient can shatter a potentially good idea. It takes work, but non-receptiveness can be remedied, if you're sold yourself.

## A SYSTEM THAT WILL MAKE YOU
## A STRONGER MANAGER

Let's steal a page from the vocational education system in the state of Georgia. In material that is given to instructors throughout the state are words of caution to help the instructors become better at their jobs.

Many of their students are disadvantaged, handicapped, school dropouts, or others who have had some successful experience in the past. One major piece of advice to the teachers is: "Get the man to compete with himself, not the other students." That means, compete for instructor's time in taking tests, in answering verbal questions, and in performance. Competition, yes—but with one's self.

It's not bad advice for a manager either. Compete first with yourself to get the very best—then turn to whipping the guy in the next department.

Here's how one girl fought the competition battle:

Mary Jane was asked by her Sunday School circle to take a spot on the program. She was to be the chairman of Bible study or some other subject. She worried about this and fretted over it. She studied and prepared herself, and one night said to me, "I just can't do it. I'm not good enough. I don't have the qualifications. They ought to get Ann Smith: she knows the Bible thoroughly. Or they should get Janie Brown: she really knows how to run a meeting." I reminded Mary Jane that they obviously wanted her for the talents that she had. If they wanted Ann Smith or Janie Brown, they would have asked them. The thing that Mary Jane had to resign herself to was the fact that she'd probably never know the Bible like Ann Smith, nor would she ever lead a meeting like Janie Brown, but that she could do both in her own style and do it adequately. A person must do things in his or her manner and to the best of his ability—not compared to someone else—and not worry that he's not as good as someone else in a certain characteristic. He proceeds to do things in the best way that he can.

A manufacturing plant uses a system called "realization," whereby a manager compares his effectiveness in using hours budgeted to him to actual hours used. He then tries to beat his own record. He is commended for improvement against his department's past performance. This is the ideal way to gauge your improvement, as opposed to trying to beat someone else. Compete with yourself first.

## HOW TO USE YOUR COMPANY'S SYSTEM TO GET THINGS DONE

In a manufacturing company the system exists to support production. No product—no jobs for anyone. Yet in many cases the system can rise up and take over and start working for itself. The industrial relations people can forget that their one goal is to get out a product—not just have a group of happy people. The finance people can get so involved in elaborate bookwork that they forget that you only need enough accounting to successfully build, sell the product, and make a profit.

One company investigated problems on the production line involving its first-level supervision. The number one problem was supervisors who did not know the scope of the system that supported them and how to make the system work for them.

Charlie Ledbetter, a manager, for example had to stop work on the line with his people, go to his office to get a labor document and take it down to Labor Relations. He had sent one copy down before without results, so he did it again. The Labor Relations Department should have been doing everything under the sun to keep him from having to leave the production line at a critical time. He could easily have exerted some pressure by phone to have someone else do his errand-running. That's why the system was set up. J. R. Brunner, on the same line, wrote a note saying he could not complete the work Labor Relations needed until they processed the letter from him. This time they did the work!

The smart manager knows how to get things done in spite of the system in many cases, but he also knows how to use it when advisable. Charles Brown, who runs a subassembly department in a manufacturing company, has posted a list of action-getters next to all of his supervisors' phones. It tells his men who to call for what. By getting with the system in a hurry, they get results in a hurry. For example, it reads:

Installing or removing a bolt . . . Tommy Patterson, Ext. 3210
Determining right size bolt . . . Floyd Stewart, Ext. 3100
Type of sealing . . . Carl Culver, Ext. 7043
Interpretation of instructions . . . Vern Davidson, Ext. 8401

and so on. These are the recurring problem areas in his shop, and these are the men he relies on. He's directing his supervisors to the quickest road for action.

Another manager, Jim Daley, also in a subassembly department, decided his machines were having too much down time. His people stood around and acted busy until machines could be fixed. This delayed his production schedule, aggravated his people and added to product costs. His first inclination was to have a troubleshooting meeting and get his supervisors together to solve the whole thing. His second thought, the one he acted on, was to get the maintenance and plant engineering people in and make them a part of the act. They came up with a better maintenance schedule, plus other ways of keeping the machines in service. They felt their responsibility. The manager was smart enough to make the system do what it was supposed to be doing. A system can work miracles. Use it, but first learn what each part does best.

## FINDING OUT WHO CAN "GET IT FOR YOU WHOLESALE"—SO YOU CAN USE THEM FOR ACTION

There are a handful of people in a large company who can do anything. I'm not talking about the president and vice president—we know they can do anything. I'm talking about people who are hidden in the organizational structure who know how to get things done. He might be head of the mail room, who knows every organization and what makes them tick. He may be a representative from Communications who knows where all the departments are. He might be the person who runs the print shop or the reproduction outfit or the staff man serving the production manager. The list goes on and varies from company to company. Learn who these people are and what they can do for you, and then get them to do it.

If you need to have a meeting outside your plant, the man from office services will run interference for you. He can get you the equipment, check out the facilities, deliver your supplies and in general set you up—if you make him do it.

A large meeting was to be held in a high school auditorium with a thousand managers and supervisors attending. The program included VIP's and other high-level personalities. Ben Alexander, manager of Quality Assurance, was asked to manage the meeting. He immediately called in three or four of the action-getting types and put them to work. The representative from office services reconnoitered the facilities and decided how the microphones should be wired, how the lights would be set, how the stage would be arranged, who would take up the tickets and how they would be handled. Another key man from public relations was asked to help with the program. He assigned time to each important speaker and had them submit a rough script to him. Ben Alexander sat back and watched all this happen. He had confidence in these men, and they delivered. He got credit for an excellent program because he was smart enough to call on the system and then let it operate. He knew the men who could get action—and he used them.

## HOW TO USE DRAMA TO CHANGE THE ATTITUDE OF THE WHOLE GROUP IF NECESSARY

John Patterson of National Cash Register Company, grandfather of modern selling, held a meeting many years ago for all of his promotion men. Its purpose was to put into effect a new sales campaign. As the program moved along, Patterson realized that it was completely over the heads of his men, but he kept working at communicating with them. When lunch time rolled around, he said, "Gentlemen, let's adjourn until nine o'clock in the morning, and I'll have a way of showing you the importance of what we're planning to do." As the men filed out of the room, one of Patterson's men came over and asked, "What do you intend to do?" He replied, "Well, I'm not going to do it, I'm going to have you men do it. By nine o'clock in the morning, I want this dining room removed."

That afternoon demolition crews came in and began removing the dining room. Late in the evening an excavation team arrived and began to fill the basement with dirt. Landscape gardeners went out into a nearby field, mowed the long grass down, snipped out the sod, loaded it onto trucks, and brought it on the site of the dining room. While the men put down the sod, a florist delivered 200 potted geraniums. In the middle of the setup, the geraniums were arranged in a star.

When Patterson's salesmen came wandering up to the meeting place the next morning, they were dumbfounded to find—instead of the dining room—a beautiful garden filled with geraniums. It cost Patterson a fortune to make this point, but his men never forgot it. He said, "Gentlemen, *anything is possible.*" He knew that an idea was no good until received by the other persons. You, as an action-getter, may need to change the attitude of a whole group. Take note of Patterson's story and use drama if necessary.

## COORDINATING ACTION CAN EVEN
## CHANGE A WHOLE TOWN

There's a quiet little town in southwest Georgia called Americus. Americus has had a population of roughly 12,000 people for many years. In the early part of the century it was a growing town. A hotel that would accommodate a much larger city was built in the middle of town. Close by—thirty miles away—the town of Albany began to grow. Americus was formerly a railroad center with all the possibilities of becoming a metropolis. However Albany overtook it and emerged a new metropolitan area with a population of 75 thousand to 100 thousand people. What happened to Americus? Only in the mid-fifties did the citizens of Americus really become disturbed that little new growth was taking place. The Jaycees, along with the Chamber of Commerce and many other civic clubs, decided that it was time to initiate some action.

Years before in Albany a tornado had wiped out the center of town and caused tremendous new building and new growth. In Gainesville, Georgia, the same thing happened. The Jaycees decided it was time for a homegrown tornado in Americus. One of the first things they did was to start a series of adult leadership classes. Nearly 150 of the top citizens in Americus were consequently stirred up and ready to get action. One result was a development corporation that promoted industry for the city. At first they attracted large mobile home manufacturers and some of their satellite industries. As the progressive atmosphere expanded, other small industries were attracted, and Americus became a growing city.

When you go into town now, you see the difference. Before the homegrown tornado, if you asked, "Where's a good place to spend the evening?" somebody would say, "Well, you ought to go on down to Albany." People are selling their city—they are selling their own facilities. The first step was changing their thinking. You may not need to change the image of a city, but you can use the same approach in changing one of your departments.

## LEARNING FROM OTHER MANAGERS

In a production plant with 30,000 employees, middle-level managers were interviewed to determine their major problems. These men were not on the first line, nor were they at the top. They were, however, the vital connecting link. Their major concern was: How can a manager make a decision that supports the total company goal and yet protects his own organization and budget? This concern, poorly handled, can lead to a crippling disease —"compartmentalization"—where each man protects his own bailiwick, even if it means less than best for the total organization. In order to be successful at this level, the manager must have the uncanny knack for tightrope-walking or juggling factors. He must have the ability to be a "swinging manager"—to swing from a decision that protects his budget one moment to a decision that meets company goal the next moment. If he dallies too long in either area the other will suffer. He must be able to analyze the variables in each managerial situation and come out with the right balance. In a classroom and in books he learns only the ideal; when he gets back on the job he finds that things don't necessarily go according to the ideal. He must learn to make trade-offs. Here's where his success begins.

What are the variables you must consider in a situation in order to make the right trade-offs and arrive at the right answer? You must be concerned with the total system. Which organizations will your decision affect? Do any of these organizations have axes to grind with you? Are there any personality conflicts? Are the right people in those organizations involved? Do you have sufficient information?

Are you emotionally involved in a way which will affect your decision? Do your employees know what to do? Is any employee emotionally involved in the situation?

The middle managers in that plant listed these as variables that they felt should be considered in order to be a successful "swinging manager."

1. Costs
2. People (reactions)
3. Other organizations affected
4. Safety
5. Material and facilities
6. Critical timing
7. Skills needed
8. Documentation needed
9. Follow-up or means of control
10. Quality
11. Customer effect
12. Responsibility limitation
13. Others

How do these match the variables in your company? Add any that you need and watch them in upcoming action-getting situations: then you can assure yourself that the action you get puts you in the best light as a manager.

Let's review some of the major considerations in developing an attitude for action:

1. Expand your confidence level by analyzing your weaknesses and accepting them.
2. Put them in proper perspective with your assets.
3. Work on improving weaknesses.
4. Work to develop an attitude demanding action.
5. Learn to give yourself a pep talk and remove negative hang-ups.
6. Use your company's "system" to get fast results.
7. Be ready to change the attitude of a group or whole department if it is necessary in order to effect a program.
8. Make trade-offs between the many management variables in order to protect your own department as well as your company.

# 2

## SURE-FIRE PRINCIPLES THAT
## GET SUCCESSFUL ACTION
## IN HANDLING PEOPLE

No matter how successful you were in improving another's attitude, don't let his enthusiasm die by doing nothing else. Keep moving! You can make one of a dozen moves that will make him act. It's like selling: the salesman makes it easy for the prospect to say "I'll buy." Make it easy for the person you're dealing with to say "I'll do," or better still, to do it.

Many principles will help you maintain momentum. Some that you will want to learn and put into practice are:

1. Schedule details that make it easy for the other person to act.
2. Get him to see action as his job.
3. Appeal to his desires.
4. Let him change his mind.
5. Handle the key person right.
6. Make the most of functional authority.
7. Keep communications open for future action.
8. Stir enthusiasm.

Let's take a look at other managers' successful application of these and other sure-fire principles.

## SCHEDULING DETAILS SO IT'S EASY
## FOR OTHERS TO ACT

There were 39 high-ranking people assembled in the room for a one-day conference and Jim Gilpin, manager of Industrial Planning, was in charge. The whole program was a gamble: if it worked, it would be a great success; if it didn't, heads would roll. High-level people from many related companies who came to the conference were going to be treated—of all things—as if they were in a conference to get action and they would *have* to participate. Almost from the start they would be broken into small groups to discuss the major problem. Beforehand several managers said, "But you don't marshall people of this level," "They may be embarrassed," and "They may refuse." Rather than quibble, Jim made the choice—that he'd get great or zero results. He selected the best, most spacious room, set up individual tables for six or seven, and put pencils and pads at each place (capitalizing on an irresistible urge to pick up a pencil and doodle which can be transformed into involvement). Coffee was available on entry. The whole atmosphere from the entrance into the room was one of participation. A few minutes were allowed for conversation at the tables.

After a short but very proper welcome, Jim presented the problem and told them, "You will discuss this at your table and define obstacles to solving the problem. You will have 15 minutes." Jim then left the room. There was an electrifying silence as it dawned on these high-level gentlemen that he meant business: he was in control and he expected action.

After 30 shattering seconds of silence, they plunged into the discussion and continued with enthusiasm the whole day. They loved being asked to participate, and the confidence of expected action was in the atmosphere. Jim knew how to schedule details so that a little action lead to a little more. Try the same with both your high- and low-level people. Schedule details to facilitate their action.

## HOW TO MAKE THE ACTION OR
## DECISION SEEM SMALL

Salesmen know how to substitute a small choice for a large one; a minor detail for a large decision; a matter of filling in information on a form—anything to keep the person from having to sit and wrestle with a major decision and come up with a negative. Take a step or two in the direction of the desired action and make it easy for the other person to complete it.

In a leading manufacturing firm, eleven departments, ranging from Tool Design to Accounts Payable, were to receive presentations honoring them for good work. This meant that the top executive, Ila Smith, would have to make many presentations. Joe Daley, Industrial Relations manager, had twice set up appointments with him to discuss details but both meetings were postponed. Finally Doug, another manager, suggested, "Listen, when you described the idea you heard Mr. Smith say that he liked it. Why don't you:

1. Call his secretary and see if he has the needed time,
2. Block out his calendar,
3. Schedule the presentations, and
4. Call the photographer.

Then when you see him, you can say, here is the plan. If he doesn't want to do it, he'll say so. Otherwise it'll be ready to go, and think of all the time you'll save him and yourself."

Doug showed Joe how to make it easy for the chief executive to act—and he did.

Why not make the decision and allow time for the other fellow to reverse it if necessary?

At another time, the top man handed a proposal to Joe and requested that he look it over. "We'll discuss plans later," he said. Joe, upon seeing the proposal, had very definite ideas as to the action needed, but was afraid that the boss wouldn't agree. To sell his idea the easy way, Joe composed a telegram outlining the action and presented it to his boss.

"Shall I send it?" he asked. It was so easy to do that his boss said "Yes" immediately. Joe scheduled action and he got it. Do as much as you can toward the action and it will seem small for the other person to complete. Action-getting has paid off for Joe. He's since moved from Industrial Relations Manager to Division Manager for Labor Relations and Employee Services, with twice the employees and a good increase in salary.

## HOW TO KEEP THE RELATIONSHIP
## SMOOTH FOR FUTURE ACTION

Leave the relationship in such good stead that you can deal effectively with the man next time. Barney, a manager in an office near me will do anything to get results—*anything,* no matter who gets sore about it! But next time around, Barney won't get cooperation because he has completely disrupted lines of communication. Get results, yes—but remember you've got to deal with people again. Each time you have to "push" somebody to get results:

- Thank the man for his help.
- Allow him to recover his ego if you push him very far.
- Allow him to win some points and be right to some extent.
- Let him feel good about the results even if you had to lead him to it.

Dwayne Young, manager of an extrusion department, had to get Bud Nolan, a representative from one of the service organizations, to devote time to a project. Dwayne forced Bud to act. He plainly told Bud he was being lax, and called several times to remind Bud of the requirements. He would not let him off the hook. In the long run, Bud did it, but he would not speak to Dwayne for several months. Dwayne then had to spend time "mending the fence." After about a half year, Bud started speaking to him and gradually reestablished a good working relationship.

There are many ways to force people without pushing them too far too fast. Keep ego in mind and gauge the push in the light of future relations. Don't disrupt them for all time.

John Ransom, assistant production manager, held a meeting of machine shop managers in a large manufacturing company. They desperately needed better service from the maintenance department, so they also invited the maintenance manager. Before the meeting John warned the other members, "Don't come down on the man personally. Don't go overboard in criticizing maintenance. Keep it on a level of asking for his help." That they did, and the maintenance manager worked hard to help clear up the situation.

Every time we deal with a person, our relationship either improves or deteriorates. It never stays the same. Leave it improved if possible.

## HOW TO USE "AGGRESSIVE" PATIENCE TO
## KEEP THINGS MOVING

John Tanner, as assistant to the president of a production company, needed to keep a close surveillance on the quality of supervision.

John had an idea for a company-wide supervisory improvement program. It needed approval by a council—at least tacit approval. The management development department had the wherewithall to plan and implement. It would be appropriate for management development to come up with the idea in the first place—for the council to recommend and approve it.

John had to plant the seeds in meetings with the group and the council. The management development group had to be challenged although they had a responsibility, as a group of experts, to originate the proposal. A meeting was called and the need was discussed, without stating a solution. At first there was a dull thud as members of the group brought out all negatives. The group considered and considered and one man ventured that "We should consider company-wide supervisory improvement, but it will have to be done immediately and that means improving 1,500 supervisors." He was told, "That's the right track, but how can we do it?" The group decided it could be done by setting up small groups of supervisors plant-wide to meet on a regular basis with a chairman. How could they be gotten to consider the topic of supervision without their being preached to? They could start by examining the labor relations problems in their groups. This could lead to looking at some other human relations problems. They then planned the mechanics of the session.

This was exactly what John wanted implemented in the first place, but *they thought of it* and they would make it work. Meanwhile, the same process went on in the council so that they recommended the same thing.

It took five times as long to arrive at the plan, but it became five times as easy to put into practice because it had been run through their thinking. Be patient and help *them* arrive at what *you* want to do. Eisenhower said, "Leadership is getting a man to do what *you* want him to do because *he* wants to do it." It takes aggressive patience to work through people, but the results are worth it.

### HOW YOU CAN GAIN COOPERATION BY APPEALING TO SOMETHING THE OTHER PERSON WANTS

There'd been bad blood between the shop managers in Catesville Mall and G. G. MacLane, the real estate manager who owned it. Constant bickering about everything from Christmas tree lights to who would connect the fountain in the Plaza had caused a complete breach. Someone had to move if the Mall was to be promoted and business brought in. The managers organized and suggested hiring a lawyer to do it for them. Warren Strand, owner of a gift shop, said, "Wait! That real estate company is basically honest. They just constantly fail to act. I have a plan." Warren called on G. G. MacLane. After listening to everything from "I got stuck at Christmas" to the preamble to the Magna Carta he stated, "Mac, your company will make an override from our sales. You need increased traffic in this shopping center. If a store fails, you must face an empty building or more expensive selling. So you stand to gain as much as we do by this promotion. Let's get together and work out a plan to 'sell' the center." MacLane said, "O.K. I'll meet you Monday." *Fait accompli!* Why? Warren considered what Mac wanted. That's a basic principle in getting action—appeal to something the other person wants. The other merchants think Warren is the smartest man on two feet when it comes to getting things done.

Too often the intense desire to get results will cause us to think only of what we want. What about the other man? He has his own wants and when he moves it will be to satisfy some of them. Why not consider these carefully and help him satisfy one or more, and in the process get results?

### USING THE DESIRES THAT PEOPLE HAVE IN COMMON

People often say, "I work with a bunch of artists. They think differently;" or "I work with men in production. They think differently." All of us have common wants. Suppose we consider these wants. Check with any of the authorities—Freud, Adler, or William James—and you will find on the top of their list of desires of every man a desire for *appreciation,* or *feeling of importance* or *recognition.* Call it what you will, it is still the self-satisfaction of being important. If you consider when it comes to changing things that everybody has this built-in desire, you can utilize it and get better results.

Dan Bruno owns and manages an art store. When he got started, he needed a great deal of help because he wasn't sure exactly what would sell. He saw that he needed the support of the art teachers at three high schools in the county, and of a couple of dozen artists in the local art colony.

Dan planned a private sneak preview and coffee for his store and invited 50 to 100 key people. This was before the store opened for business. He asked each to jot down suggestions for the store. The artists were pleased, the high school teachers were pleased and, best of all, Dan was pleased. He had made them feel important and had done it sincerely. They won't trade anywhere else. In fact, the teachers now call him before they start a class to see that he is stocked up.

The key was that Dan appealed to their importance. It is a desire we have in common. So if you are ever in doubt as to what moves the other man, keep this in mind. It can get results.

## HELPING HIM SEE THE ACTION YOU WANT AS A PART OF HIS JOB

Harvey Daleman was head of a finance department. Tom Coyle, his assistant finance manager called a meeting of representatives on an issue that was part of their job obligation. "I had 12 of 18 representatives present," Harvey fumed. One third of his committee representing all finance departments didn't feel it was worthwhile to attend the meeting and didn't even feel compelled to tell him why.

Tom complained, "Enthusiasm is waning in our organization." Why not? He was the culprit. It seemed that Tom had communicated the unimportance of the meeting; he had communicated a "why bother" or an "if you don't have anything else to do" attitude to his people, so you couldn't blame them.

When Harvey questioned Tom about this sort of attendance, Tom said, "Aw, you always shoot for 100 percent."

Harvey roared, "You're darned right! Every man who doesn't attend the meeting after he's committed is expected to have an A-1 excuse or a written note from his mother. His presence is needed or he wouldn't be on the committee. If he's got a thousand other things to do, don't ask him to serve on a committee for kicks. If he's needed, he's needed; so he's expected to attend."

After this lecture from Harvey, Tom went back and wrote a memo to all involved managers: "Your man will be there, or I should know why, or change men." At the next meeting he had to send out for chairs.

It's critical that the people working for you understand that you're not buying their time, but productivity of some sort—the results of applying their time. To assure that your organization gets what it deserves you must make any one who deals with it feel the same. Let the individual know that action is expected as a part of his job.

## THE SECRET OF GETTING ENTHUSIASM

Roy Stratford, production manager of an assembly plant, was having a bad time with one of his men who criticized the electrical wiring department. Everything that came out was wrong, or he didn't like it for some reason. Roy put him in that department as manager and before long things changed. When this manager was later transferred to another organization, he became a most enthusiastic promoter of the electrical wiring department. He understood its workings and felt a part of it.

When the city of Americus had the promotion for the leadership training as discussed in Chapter 1, no one outside of the training program promoted it. How could a man promote an idea he didn't think enough of to investigate? On the other hand, if he knew about it, he could sell it with authority and enthusiasm.

According to the Greeks enthusiasm means "God within us." That's pretty strong stuff, but I guess that's why it gets action—and it does. How do you get enthusiasm? Well, one way is by ensuring that the other person is thoroughly sold on the idea or action. Maybe he sees a way to get something he wants; maybe he has to do something to help develop the idea or maybe he participates in even a minor part of the action.

However your man comes to a task, get him involved so he has a stake in the outcome! Enthusiasm comes from within: that's where the action must also begin.

## HOW TO MAKE IT EASY FOR HIM TO CHANGE HIS MIND TO YOUR WAY OF THINKING

While touring Italy last summer, Jane Rowe decided to purchase a piece of Venetian glass. She chose an expensive item and paid duty for it to be imported. When she got back to this country, the package arrived and to her horror she found the wrong bowl in it. Jane felt that she had been gypped and she was furious.

She sat down and wrote a letter that let the fire in her mind show. She then let the letter cool off for a day or two and decided to rewrite it.

Jane began the letter: "While touring your enjoyable country last August, I had the pleasure of visiting Venice and your shop. There I purchased a . . ." and she went on to explain. Then she stated "It was an unavoidable error"—and later: "knowing you will want to do the right thing . . ." Toward the end, instead of saying, "You people will pay the expense of having the wrong item sent back and the new one sent over," she said, "I'm sure you will be willing to pay the expense of exchanging items."

Within a matter of weeks, she received a letter from Venice agreeing with everything she said: apologizing for the mistake and saying that the correct bowl would be rushed to her immediately. In addition, since the cost of return mailing was so great, they offered to let her buy the other bowl at half price. They were bending over backwards to make good their mistake.

That's how easy it is to let someone change his mind to your way of thinking. As managers, we may use the same technique.

One of Socrates' favorite methods of changing attitudes was

through agreement. As he wandered around the streets of Athens where many people opposed his views, one of the ways he sold his opinions was by getting a man to agree on a familiar thought. Then he pursued another thought and got agreement, and gradually moved to the new area of thinking. The man was ready to agree because his mind had been led in a process of positive responses. Often a man can change his opinion if he is put in an agreeable mood. As a manager, part of your job is getting people to change their minds. Here are some tips to help you:

—Don't insult them personally.
—Don't infer that they would do wrong intentionally.
—Don't challenge what they say or do, so that they can't back up.
—Don't impugn their honor; in other words, leave them a way out or as the Orientals say, "Help them save face".

## REFUSING ANYTHING LESS THAN RESULTS, NO MATTER HOW LOGICAL THE EXCUSE

If you've ever built a house, opened a store, extended a business, or had any construction work done, you can write this chapter yourself, provided you are still sane. Transfer a lesson from that experience to any dealing with people.

Several years ago, we built a new house. My wife was extremely proud of the fact that she was getting a slate floor in the entry hall. She was very particular about the color and the placement of the slate.

She was fighting mad when I came home one day. "Come out here and look at my entry hall," she said. Sure enough, the painters had painted the walls and dripped paint all over the slate. I told her to call them, tell them to come back and clean up the mess. She did.

However, when I came home again after they had finished the cleaning, she said, "Come and look." This time they had not really cleaned the slate; they merely smeared the paint and left. I told her to call once more and get them to try again.

On the third try the men managed to smear cleaning fluid around the edge of the wall and ruin the paint job. I told my wife to call them and get them to do the paint job over. They did it exactly! They slopped paint all over the slate floor again. Four tries later, the same situation existed because of sloppy service!

We didn't stop. We kept on until we got the floor cleaned. It is necessary to demand service in conjunction with getting action. The weak falter and pay dearly. We must learn to get what we pay for. We must learn to get it from people who work for us and from people who coordinate with us. Ask that any work or service be done over to your satisfaction even if it means doing it again and again.

## STICK BY YOUR GUNS UNTIL YOU GET ACTION

Herb Jones told me that he's learned to stick by his guns.

Herb bought an Xmobile. At 24,000 miles the whole transmission fell apart: a line sprung a leak and the fluid drained out.

Herb called the car company. They said, "Sorry, but the warranty is only good for 24,000 miles. Talk to the corporation." The corporation said to talk to the dealer. The ball went back and forth.

After twelve calls, the corporation and dealer saw that Herb wasn't going to give up. Never did Herb raise his voice. His words were always challenging but, at the same time, always positive: "in the name of your reputation," etc. He knew he was right and that he wasn't going to pay even if he had to call a vice president in Detroit. Courteous determination paid off—and so did the auto company.

Herb's persistence won. If you're right, don't give up—don't give in. Don't stop short of complete satisfaction—but do it cooly and courteously. Above all, don't lose your temper unless you do it in a calculated manner.

Don't let the other fellow's run-around derail you. Refuse anything less than the results you want—stick by your guns.

Perhaps the name of this section ought to be "persistence."

Remember the story of Warren and the real estate manager. Every other store owner had given up dealing with the manager because he was never in the office and never returned their calls when he came in. What did Warren do? At 1:45 PM he started calling person to person. The manager was on another phone; he left a number. At 2 PM there was no return call, Warren placed the person-to-person call again. Warren continued this every 15 minutes until 3:30 when he got through. The real estate manager realized that Warren was not to be turned off. An effective manager can't afford to be turned off if he's right and intends to get action—so stick to your guns.

## HOW TO HANDLE THE KEY PERSON WHO'LL GET RESULTS FROM THE TOP MAN

Is the controlling factor the boss's secretary? His administrative assistant? His staff man? Who has the key?

Steve Hale, sales manager of Ogilvie Produce needed to get in to talk with the manager of a large marketing association. Others had struck out here but Steve had to try his hand.

His first and most important step was to contact the receptionist and ask the secretary's name. Then he called her and said, "Alice, this is Steve Hale, with Ogilvie Produce. I'd like to talk with your manager about how we can help him. But I need some information. Can you tell me how many men he has working for him? and _____ and _____?"

Alice was pleased at his knowing her name. She was pleased at his knowing how important she was. She not only gave him the information but set up an appointment and helped him get what he wanted.

Defer to the influence of key persons and they'll throw their weight around on your side.

## DETERMINING THE IMPORTANCE OF PEOPLE-DEALING IN YOUR MANAGEMENT

There are two major approaches to getting the most from people: force and persuasion.

In applying force, we rely on a man doing a job because a person with authority tells him to. The key factor here is that his job is at stake: if he doesn't do something, he's fired. There is fear to consider in using force. The other approach is one of persuasion, or selling, which means appealing to an individual and causing him or her to want to do something.

One approach relies entirely on the flow of authority; the other, on motivation through personal selling, regardless of authority.

Let's consider the first approach. A young supervisor, Joe Doyle, had trouble with some of his employees. He called Sam into the office and discussed the difficulty. In no uncertain terms Joe told Sam that he would have to improve or else. Sam alternated between tears and anger, left the office—and improved. This is one case where a chewing-out worked. Why? Sam was obstinate, loud and brash. He had been warned before and was huffy. There are limited times when nothing beats an effective dressing down and this was one of them. But any manager who relies on this as his standard approach is doomed to failure. Joe knew that Sam needed this particular kind of handling, yet if he handled everybody that way, he would be wrong. Joe must be able to vary his approach to suit the situation. Luckily, he can. Try both of these approaches to people-dealing and arrive at your own best technique. But begin by assuring yourself that a knowledge of handling people effectively will be your key to getting action.

Note what turned up in one large industry:

An executive development session was attended by all of the managers of a major organization. During the session, these men had to rate each other on many of their qualities. They were men who were not just casually associated: most of them had worked with each other for 10 to 15 years and knew each other thoroughly.

Two men ranked high in people-dealing, but lowest in technical knowledge. Two other men came out very high in technical knowledge and very low in people-dealing. Within six months, the two who were high in people-dealing had moved up one notch in their jobs. The two who were rock bottom in that quality had moved down a peg; in fact, one finally left the company. In this experience, people-dealing was the top priority skill.

Really sell yourself on the importance of knowing how to handle people. It's far easier to do technical work and to hire people with technical ability than it is to find a man adroit in managing people. Make it a top priority for your men.

## SUCCESSFUL WAYS TO DEAL UP THE LINE

In the executive development session mentioned earlier, another experiment was tried. Each manager was asked to handle three human relations situations. Each situation called for correction of a fault in another individual—without having the other explode. In one case, the subject assumed he was dealing with somebody working directly *below him*. In the next case, he would be dealing with somebody across the line on an *equal level*, but not in his own organization. In the third case, he was asked to talk with *his boss* about correcting a fault. It was found that in correcting someone down the line, the supervisor found it very easy to be blunt and completely honest, and to discount any of the desires of the individual. The second situation found the man using a little more tact and salesmanship as he talked to someone across the line. He gave more consideration and was a little more cautious; he considered the other individual. In the third situation, when he was talking up the line, he began pussyfooting. He not only was soft spoken but used every human relations rule he knew. When he realized he had built-in authority, one thing happened. When he realized that he was going upstream, another; and across the line, yet another. If the manager handling the situation were really concerned with the other individual as a human being and not as a tool in his hands, then he would consider every man the same. It is pretty hard to convince a manager to do this. I'm not saying everyone should be handled the same, but that we should be aware that we change our direction because of rank or authority and not because of individual personality needs.

Here are some ideas:

- —If the atmosphere is such that a man likes to be called by his first name, call him by his first name the first time you ever meet him—then do it every time you see him.
- —Always defer to rank. But don't kowtow to it. People love to be treated like human beings.
- —Be considerate of your prospect's time and get on with your work and out of his way. If you have a long session, feel him out along the line to see if you're imposing.

—Above all else, act with confidence in dealing with him; that's what he's paying you for.

## HOW TO USE FUNCTIONAL AUTHORITY AND GET ACTION ACROSS THE LINE

A small manufacturing plant employing about 500 people had a high degree of interpersonal and functional interface between various functions and levels of management. All members of management appeared to be dedicated to doing a good job. The plant still had growing pains from expansion last year (both in operator effectiveness and management systems) and these two areas of concern reflected themselves in costs, schedule, and quality. Supervision seemed at times to work around the system rather than through it—a combination of not knowing the system itself and not knowing how to make the system work. The management group was eager to strengthen its management team effectiveness for the attainment of organizational goals. The management team wanted to tighten up its management controls, particularly in the fabrication, use and accountability of tools and fixtures.

The managers were asked by their president to define the reasons they don't get results. They cited poor communications, lack of clear-cut goals, lack of follow-up on corrective actions, failure to create interest and desire for excellence among personnel, insufficient team work, lack of order and organization, insufficient interest and support from other organizations, and failure to delegate responsibility. It was a hot bed where functional authority needed to be operating at its best.

Into this mess stepped Herm Neal. As head of manufacturing engineering, he drew up a plan for controlling work flow, supplies and parts. Instead of selling it, he tried to force it. He left in a heat!

John Cowart succeeded with almost the same plan, but he

a. Got to know each affected individual.
b. Showed an eager interest in them.
c. Explained simply the needed changes and interface from department to department.

d. Praised the slightest improvement any individual or department made.

e. Gave others credit for the changes.

He knew how to sell himself and how to praise, so he came through a winner. The employees thought he was great and management got their changes.

If you're going across lines, take time to sell your plan and gain acceptance. Even if it's a little slower, it is the only force you have and can be enough to do a functional job.

## KEEPING THE LINE OPEN FOR INCOMING MESSAGES THAT CAN INFLUENCE YOUR DIRECTION

Your drive for action must be strong, but if you close communications in the process then you may miss your target.

Joe May got a call from one of his men in the data collection center of a shipping company. Joe, fortunately, is a smart enough manager to help get his man out of a jam. Joe's man, Bill, stated, "Come out here and let me show you where the system doesn't work." When he arrived, it was easy for Joe to see that his assistant and the clerk were furious.

Bill said, "They won't take this form and process it." The clerk stated, "We are not supposed to take it. It's supposed to be on an XYZ form." Bill then pulled out a procedure that seemed to support him.

"Let's go to the office and study it," suggested Joe and told the clerk not to worry about it and they'd let him know later.

Sure enough, the clerk was right. When they went back and told him so, he beamed as if to say "I told you so." But then he immediately went to work helping get the right form and the report submitted. He couldn't do enough for them.

But a few more minutes with Bill earlier would have closed the door forever. Joe knows how to keep communication going with an individual even though the exchange is hot. You might need a man to finalize the action, so keep the lines open.

Perhaps the most important points made in this chapter are:

1. Put people dealing first on your list of management skills.
2. Try several ways to arrive at your own best style.
3. Stick by your guns until you get results.
4. Keep your relationship on a good enough basis for results this time and in the future.

# 3

## DEFINING ASSIGNMENTS TO GET ACTION AND CLEAR-CUT RESULTS

If your instructions for a particular assignment are misunderstood, it's your fault. No matter how smart or dumb the other man may be, you take the blame. Many cases of action missed or results poorly delivered stem from lack of a meeting of the minds.

In your position as an action-getting manager, you've got to be better than the rest. Let's see how you can up your batting average.

Your language must be simple and understandable.
Each assignment should be broken into simple steps, if necessary.
Each step should be discussed in key points.
Steps should be sequenced.
You should be sure that your man has the right equipment or can get it.
You should whet his enthusiasm and see that he understands the assignment before leaving it to him.

At the moment, we're only talking about defining the assignments. We'll talk about getting action which is up to your exact standards later. Here's a closer look at the specifics you'll need to pay attention to in assigning for results.

## HOW PAYING ATTENTION TO DETAILS
## HELPS YOU COLLECT TARGETED RESULTS

A couple of weeks before Christmas, a young woman sat down to wrap presents with her little daughter. Betsy, eight years old, wrapped a present for her school teacher—a couple of candles in glass containers. Her mother wrapped a present for Betsy's uncle.

They delivered the present to the teacher and after returning home that evening, they were looking at the packages still to be delivered. Betsy's mother looked at the present to her brother and exclaimed, "Something is wrong!" She opened it and found the two candles.

"Good grief," she cried, "This is the present for the teacher." And then it dawned on her that at that very moment, the teacher had a lovely package from little Betsy containing a fifth of bourbon!

They raced to the teacher's home in time to swap the packages . . . before the teacher had opened hers. (If she'd had a chance to open it, she might have been a little disappointed at the swap.)

The mother almost got in trouble for not paying attention to details; so do managers.

Some men can glean details from chaos like a gleaner gleans wheat from chaff. Take Jake Parker, for example, an administrative supervisor for an electronics company. When the company decided to market some of the small products that they had been making for internal use, the boss asked several people to investigate and give ideas.

Then one day they met and it was pandemonium. Everyone had a different idea and a different approach. Some discussed one responsibility and some another. The boss made no move. Jake stood it as long as he could and then he jumped up to the board and said, "Wait a minute. Let's see where we stand. Jim, you suggested XY product. Sam, you suggested YZ. Joe, you YW. Let's write them down." Which he did. Then he said, "Jim, you be ready to report at the next meeting how we can market XY product. Sam, you YZ, etc . . ." He clarified the situation, let each person know his responsibility and changed a melee into orderly assignments. In later sessions the product was decided.

As a result, Jake was given the job of marketing supervisor with several men reporting to him. His paying attention to and defining details opened a whole new field for him.

You can't afford confusion in your assignments. Just as Jake clarified, you also must ensure that your men know exactly what their assignments are and what is expected. If you are to get targeted results, be sure all details spell out the target for each man.

### CHOOSING WORDS THAT MAKE YOUR INSTRUCTIONS EASY TO UNDERSTAND

My friend Kenneth speaks gobbledegook: two-thirds of what he says in meetings I don't understand. I'm sure that nobody else in the meeting understands either. Kenneth goes to great length and great detail to use abbreviations—for one thing. Instead of General Dynamics, he says GD. Instead of saying Logistics, he says LOG. By the time he puts them all together, you've got abbreviation after abbreviation and it sounds like an unknown tongue.

The only way I can analyze this, since he obviously is not considering his listener, is that he is either trying to get attention, trying to sound smart, or is just oblivious to how little the people around him understand what he is saying.

Fortunately, you're smarter than Ken and in order to avoid his gobbledegook trap, you can check your instructions:

1. Am I considering the other fellow's understanding, not my own?
2. Do the words mean the same to him as they do to me?
3. Do they adequately describe my requirements?
4. Is there any way in which they're ambiguous?

Here's how one fast thinker caught a double meaning and won. Tom Ritter, engineer in a chemical company, sat down at the club to chat with an acquaintance, Jim McLendon. Jim owned a small clothing plant, manufacturing ladies wear and also has a small farm producing acres of high-grade corn. They talked about clothing and Jim's work until Tom changed the subject.

"Our potash will help your plant," Tom stated. Jim did a double-take and said, "I don't understand." Then Tom realized he had made several communications errors. He had jumped ahead of the conversation and was thinking of Jim's corn plants, and he had inadvertently used the singular rather than the plural. After Tom made his meaning clear, Jim invited him out to the farm and gave him a contract for the potash.

Tom shrewdly evaluated his words and made them clear. You need a constant reading of your own language to be sure that your meaning is clear and that you are being understood.

## HOW TO MAKE AN ASSIGNMENT APPETIZING AND BOOST ENTHUSIASM

Some words carry a stigma. Can't you smell the "stench" of garbage? However, because of advertising, can't you almost enjoy the "aroma" of tobacco? You can tell a man he's trim, but not skinny. Husky or stocky, but not fat. Words arouse. What has this got to do with action? *Choose your words carefully.*

A person may not be "wrong"—he may only be "looking at it in a different light." You don't in many cases "disagree"; you take a "slightly different view." A word isn't necessarily "sorry;" it "could be better" or "isn't as good as the person usually does."

Use verbs that plant the seed of an idea or feeling. Don't say "you are going to take the following trips," but "you are going to enjoy the following trips." In other words, make it appetizing.

Suppose you have given an unusually hard job to Joe. Tell him so. You might say, "Joe, I know this is a hard one and that's why I gave it to you; I knew you could handle it." He'll thrive.

Or let him know it is a challenge: "Joe, this one will really test you, but I know it won't throw you."

It might be something he isn't used to doing and you feel it'll help him develop: "Joe, this assignment will help you grow in a new area."

Your expression of confidence and challenge can help make a hard job appetizing and boost his enthusiasm for completing it successfully.

## HOW TO BREAK A JOB INTO STEPS FOR
## CLEAR ASSIGNMENTS

Suppose you were made manager of a brand new department. This might be ideal in seeing that things happen right from the beginning.

—Define clearly all of the duties and responsibilities of your whole department.
—Apportion these to your supervisors and define where one's responsibility begins and the other's ends.
—Make sure each supervisor takes over to see that the job assignments are broken down for individual employees.

Your supervisor may spell out the technical job duties as Willie Mathias did for his men. Willie is in an engineering organization and his group is responsible for Finishes and Processes. He listed the general job duties of one of his development engineers this way:

Responsible to supervisor for completing design activities in manufacturing, purchasing, quality support for finishes and processes. Review and coordinate with other engineers in similar duty.
1. Give guidance and information related to finishes and processes to organizations to influence new designs or changes.
2. Review all designs to see that they conform with already established requirements.
3. Keep up-to-date information on materials and processes through periodicals, monitoring tests, seminar attendance, and contact with associated agencies.
4. Direct specifications for use of any materials on company products.
5. Update design handbook for company.
6. Do any miscellaneous assignments given by group engineer.

As you might suspect, Willie's group has a reputation as the most efficient group in the company. It's his clear job definition that has helped bring this about.

Let's go to another field to look at one simplified task and how it can be defined. Suppose you are managing a department in a store that has several groups engaged in making sales. You want to have your supervisors spell out duties to each clerk and then break down tasks accordingly. Take the simple task of writing a sales ticket using a credit card. You may have each supervisor describe the job this way:

Step 1. Verify price.
Step 2. Put it on sales ticket.
Step 3. Put taxes on ticket.
Step 4. Put sales check in machine with credit card and stamp.
Step 5. Phone credit office to verify.
Step 6. Have customer sign.

You broke the job into its simplest parts. Each part may require certain knowledge to perform. Even that knowledge can be spelled out:

A. How to arrive at price if it's not on article.
B. How to figure taxes.
C. Who is authorized to approve credit and how you show it on ticket.

Each step may require that certain time or quality standards be met. This will be discussed in a later chapter. For the time being we're concerned just with the steps that make up a total.

Your knowledge of the man and the job will determine how far you go in outlining steps. If he's brilliant and experienced, he might be insulted if you decide it in very simple steps. On the other hand, lacking any proof to the contrary, you should assume he knows nothing about the job and make it easy.

## HELPING HIM TO BRIDGE ANY STEPS THAT HE DOESN'T NEED TO TAKE

Any steps in his assignment that he can skip will save you and him just that much more time. For example:

—Why let him research a project when someone else has done it previously?
—If a carbon copy isn't going to be used, then don't expect him to make one.

—If someone else is running a credit check on the company, although he would ordinarily do this, skip it.

—If another department is ordering computer printout, use theirs and save another run.

If it isn't really necessary, skip it, and continue with the next step. One advantage in laying out an assignment by steps is to see what can be eliminated or bridged.

## DEFINING KEY POINTS THAT WILL MAKE EACH STEP SUCCESSFUL

He needs certain information—certain parameters—to make the most of each step. Either you must define this information or know that he knows it. Put yourself in the manager's shoes in the following situations:

You're in the Marketing Research Department and you're assigning an update on a vital report.

—One step is "request data printout of data processing department." Key points associated with this step are: instruct Scientific Computing to use multilith masters only, to use a new ribbon and run machine at reduced speed.

—Another step is "request for date change on report cover." Key points are: to instruct Special Arts to change date on cover, binding, and title page

These are samples of the information your man must have in order to complete the steps successfully. If he's experienced he will know these points. If not, he needs your help in spelling them out.

Your secretary is going to program a letter in a flexowriter machine.

—Step one is putting paper in the machine. She must know to use two sheets.

—Step two is setting the margin. She must know there is no right margin and how to compensate.

*Or:*

Your supervisor is assigning a tune-up mechanic to clean an auto and replace sparkplugs.

—He is going to regap the plug. To do it he must know how to use a gapping tool. He must also know how to file electrodes.

Consider what information a person must know or have access to in order to be successful in handling a job, step by step. Can you give it to him? Will he need to search it out himself? This is another safeguard in making successful assignments.

## SEQUENCING YOUR INSTRUCTIONS FOR MAXIMUM UNDERSTANDING

Suppose the man repairing shoes attaches the heel before he puts on the sole? He's got trouble!

Suppose you sign a lease before the loan you need goes through?

Suppose you design a rack without first determining the load it will carry?

Somebody goofed. There's a natural order to processes and there should be an obvious order to your instructions. By spelling out items as they are due, we not only set priorities but also help with understanding the total assignment.

Jake Parker, the administrative supervisor discussed earlier, is also a master at sequencing. He'll state that on March 3 Plan 1 will be ready for final writing, Plan 2 will be in the hands of the editors, and Plan 4 will be in the art department. He plots each move months ahead if necessary so that each person knows when a certain bit of work reaches a certain point. That's planning in sequence!

In mass production a set-back chart shows what has to happen before each part comes into being. These can be assembled to make a larger part, which is assembled with others to make a final product. The set-back chart represents sequencing at its ultimate.

Carlton Turner, manager of a manufacturing company, increased output 30 percent by improving the sequencing of instructions. His assignment was to ensure correctness of shop orders. He gave these instructions to all of his people:

1. Check part number on variable portion of the shop order.
2. Initial top left hand corner of shop order.
3. Punch shop order control center cards and work orders.
4. Move shop order and cards to set-up desk, etc.

The result was a thirty percent increase in productivity! Consider carefully whether your men can see a logical order in any instructions or assignments. If not, put it there quickly.

### SPELLING OUT YOUR REQUEST IN TERMS THAT CLINCH THE DEAL

What'll it take to really pin your request down? Might take a little common sense as well as the right details.

Twelve men sat in a meeting room making final plans for the test flight of a small plane. The press and the public were to be invited. Refreshment stands were to be set up. Suddenly the thought struck the men, "Suppose it rains Saturday?"

"If it rains we'll have to postpone it," said one of the leaders. "In fact, I'll call the weather bureau on Friday. If they say 50-50 chance of rain, I'll call it off. If they say 20 percent chance, I think we'll go ahead. If they say 40 percent, I think we should call it off. If they . . ."

Whereupon a wise old manager with more common sense than the man speaking piped up with, "Aw, Sam, if a lot of people say it's gonna rain like hell, call it off." That's common sense.

Frank Jenkins took a writer on a tour of his savings and loan association. "You ought to write a part of the article for the paper," was a casual remark made by the writer. "Yeah," Frank replied. Two weeks later came the ultimatum, "Where's the article?" Poor Frank honestly did not know that he had made a commitment that should have been honored. The fellow at the other end of the conversation thought he had communicated. He's going to stay in trouble unless he improves his terms. The writer should have told Frank or anyone else the date he needed the article and the form it should have been in. Nothing helps clinch a deal better than specifics such as when something is due, in what form, where, and by whom. Follow these specifics with your request and you'll stay in the action-getting ranks.

## HOW TO USE DRAMA TO GET HIS
## COMPLETE ATTENTION

A letter arrived in my office from a vice president. It was traumatic. I haven't stopped shaking yet. Yet it was a nice letter: typewritten and polite, addressed to me personally, and in an envelope marked "personal." It asked me to help cut down on long distance phone calls. My secretary and I immediately pleaded guilty. We could have saved money and we knew it. What about that call to Boston? A letter would have sufficed. Couldn't we have wired the professor in Michigan? We decided to throw ourselves on the mercy of the court. This letter had impact and made us stop and think. In other words, it got action. It was one of dozens of management directives we receive each month, yet it avoided the standard channels of communication. It made the message stand out.

Later I learned that *every person approved for outside calls received the same letter*, and I'm sure each person was as much affected by the message as I was. We have a shook-up organization, but everyone is conscious of cutting long distance calls.

To get action in a memo, let's ask ourselves what can be done to distinguish and impress the importance of the message. Raise your message out of the ordinary like the vice president did with the personal address. Address it in your own handwriting; mention the reader's specific situation; have it hand delivered. Anything to distinguish it will get the receiver's attention.

Joe Lydon, as a new manager in the spare parts division of a company, took over responsibilities for physical inventory. Some of the factors to be considered were: (1) Kardex file in the department enabled supervisors to have control and knowledge of where and how much stock was supposed to be on hand. (2) Personnel turnover in the group had been over 50 percent. (3) No procedure in inventory accounting was available. (4) Increased emphasis was placed on strict inventory control by top management.

Joe had never been through an inventory before and took strict steps. He wrote out a procedure and sprinkled pictures throughout. These were given to each person doing the work. A brief but thorough meeting was held to go over all points. Questions were answered. Results: everyone got the same picture and started on the same wavelength. The company finance manager commented that it was the best inventory ever held. The error rate was only 1.9% on 4,368 items. Joe received a commendation from his manager for his effective handling of the inventory. Joe recommends visual aids and discussions—write it down and talk it up.

Don't be afraid to do something different if it will help to assure that your instructions are understood, starting with making sure that you have complete and undivided attention.

## CHECKING HIS UNDERSTANDING OF THE ASSIGNMENT BEFORE YOU LEAVE IT WITH HIM

Joe, in the last example, not only dramatized with pictures, but saw that each person understood before leaving the meeting. There are many ways to accomplish this, but nothing beats having it in writing.

A group of store owners met to plan a Mother's Day promotion. Everybody described a different plan, ranging from the sublime to the ridiculous. Everybody talked at once. Two days later no one was sure exactly what had happened at the meeting. The next time the owners met, one man started writing down assignments and deadline dates: (1) Jay contact the newspaper by Monday, (2) Mary get the posters Tuesday, (3) Ed get the tickets ready for Saturday, etc. When the meeting was over, the secretary was asked to copy this and hand it out to each person. Understanding was complete.

Write down any instructions if possible. A man can slough off verbal instructions, but a written note is like having chewing gum stuck in the palm of your hand—you can't shake it off. It is there to haunt you and you feel compelled to take action with it.

Henry, a display designer, was putting a floor display together.

Bart, a technician, told Henry twice, "That isn't a very effective slogan in the display. In fact, it is really inaccurate."

Each time Henry said, "Uh huh," and added, "How do you like the red, white and blue borders?" or "Isn't the model in a fine location?"

All indications showed he wasn't getting the point . . . "Change it." Bart kept pleading. Unfortunately Bart had no absolute authority to tell Henry to change it. Finally Bart spoke to the man who could get action, Henry's floor manager.

He repeated his warning, "That slogan is inaccurate," and explained why.

"Yeah," the floor manager said, "I'll see that it is changed." And it was.

That's action. We can't be satisfied to say, "Well, I told him." Not when it's action we need. All sights and sounds must point to his taking action. The most useless words when something goes wrong are: "Well, I told him." Either you didn't communicate or you weren't believed. You should have gotten it changed or other results. Check his understanding before leaving it with him.

## DECIDING HOW MUCH RESEARCH IS JUSTIFIED

When do you stop looking and get the job done? Engineers are famous for having to be called to a halt. After all, they are hired to design the best, and how do you know when that point has been reached? A design can be done over and over again without ever being sure it is the best. How long can a man gather facts and information before he settles down to solve the problem? At some time he must stop gathering and start delivering.

Just as in sequencing instructions, time can be set up in the beginning of a project or assignment to gather information, if original information is needed. However, a due date needs to be assigned, and at least a relative time set by which work must be started. For example, if you want a report in three weeks, you may require the first draft by the end of 10 days. This means research and draft can't take longer. If the worker wants to take several cuts at it, he still must have the draft at the set date.

Mike Agricola manages 10 artists in an art department. He may be called on for a safety poster, an equal employment poster, or a newspaper advertising layout. Whenever he passes along an assignment, he asked for suggested layouts or rough ideas. These are due two days later. He then allows six days to put it into good form to show the Division Manager. He allows two more days for rework and resubmittal and then meets the due date on the button. But he allows the artist two days in the beginning to cogitate and research rough ideas.

No matter what the assignment, it is worthwhile to consider time for research, rough plans or designs and necessary changes while there's still time to finish the final product.

## HOW TO TIE IN WITH SOMETHING HE ALREADY KNOWS FOR ADDITIONAL CLARITY AND RESULTS

Joe Turbelow, a methods manager in an assembly plant, was asked to speak to a group of visiting students. His assignment was to explain the function of the Methods and Planning Department. How did it relate to Engineering? How did it relate to Manufacturing? Joe told the group that his department's function was like the neck of an hour glass. Engineering was like the top portion where everything originates; manufacturing, the destination, was like the bottom part. It all goes through the neck to get there. The students understood the relationship instantly because it was explained in terms they already understood—an excellent analogy.

In giving an assignment, Bob Harrison, a supervisory training manager, draws on a person's previous knowledge. When a Job Corps contract was in the offing he had to decide who he would send to Washington to get the bidding information. He sent Howard Bibb, who had worked with an underprivileged manpower program the year before and was familiar with many of the circumstances that were the same for the Job Corps. Howard listened to briefings and picked up the contract information that helped turn in a winning proposal.

Bob got a contract by drawing on something Howard already knew. In giving assignments you improve your action-getting chances if you tie in to previous knowledge or accomplishment.

## MAKING SURE HE HAS THE RIGHT EQUIPMENT AND KNOWLEDGE CAN PREVENT TIME-CONSUMING DELAYS

One advantage in having to consider the steps required in completing an assignment is that it's easier to see that equipment and materials are available.

> Your man has to prepare Materials and Process Reports (as discussed earlier). He must assemble all necessary information to convey understanding to individuals unfamiliar with the problems. This means writing and rewriting. Who will do it? There is a group whose job is to type up such reports. Be sure he knows about them and he can avoid tying up himself and your secretary when they should be doing higher priority work.

Jim Monroe, sales manager in a manufacturing company, is careful that any presentation that his men plan is keyed to available equipment. If slides are to be used he makes sure that lead time is available to get them from the photographic department. If a movie to show the product in action is needed, he secures preliminary approval from top management before planning. If handouts are used, he makes sure they are planned, printed, and delivered to him two days before the presentation. Check with the man to whom you give an assignment and be sure that he has the right materials and equipment. If not, allow time in the assignment for it to arrive.

There's one guy that I used to work with who insisted on telling everything he knows when telling you how to do something. He gets satisfaction out of his knowledge. But the other fellow's understanding is sacrificed in the process.

Jim Titson teaches in a technical school. If a student needs to know how to read a scale, he is taught only when it is necessary. Jim doesn't teach the student math or algebra—just how to read a scale. That's functional instruction.

Glen Morris, division manager for a chain of stores, had to train Sara White, a new store manager. Sara needed to know prices, buying, stocking and many other aspects of store operation. She also needed to know how to operate a cash register. For her first time on the register, Glen merely taught her how to push the right buttons and make change. He showed her next how to change dates and verify sales on the memory tape. Later he showed her how to change the memory tape and the receipt tape. He knew she couldn't master all the mechanics of the machine at one sitting, so he broke it down into segments and gave only enough information at each step to do the job. This avoided confusion.

Decide how much is necessary for a particular part of the job and stop there. A person can retain and use just so much. Massive instructions lead to massive confusion. Keep it simple and get results.

## HOW TO POINT OUT POSSIBLE PITFALLS AHEAD OF TIME AND GET AROUND THEM

You are manager of the Personnel Section and currently processing 20 to 50 people per day. Your clerks and supervisors must keep control of the paper work and see that action is taken in each individual case. You've long since learned that Jake Thompson, the head of Industrial Planning, is slow. When you break in a new person one of the things you tell him is Jake Thompson moves slowly. When your new person sends a requisition to him for review and approval, he should follow up the next day. If he doesn't, it will stagnate, and your client will suffer.

Jack Standish heads a Materials Purchasing Department and has four supervisors and 28 people working for him. When he knows which company responds rapidly and which bogs down he tells his people this. He warns that X company uses up all of the extra time and then comes in late. The only way to do business with them and meet your commitments is to push them early. This is just one pitfall that he warns his people about and helps them avoid.

We learn by our errors, but it can cost time and money. Let others learn from your experience and avoid any known pitfalls.

Let's restate. In defining assignments clearly for results, keep things simple. Break down into steps or stages. Work on your man's enthusiasm, and be sure necessary equipment or material is available.

# 4

# HOW TO SET STANDARDS THAT GUARANTEE SUCCESSFUL PERFORMANCES

Making someone else know what you call good is like feeling a rainbow. Managers fail everyday because they can't describe what they want and when. Let's learn how to set standards and guarantee a successful performance. That means defining quality, time factors, cost and even the personal quirks of a manager that may trap an employee.

You may be a result-getter, but are the results what you want? Do you accept what is given by the performer and bend your standards to fit it, or do you really make the person meet your standards?

Many industries have huge quality control or quality assurance organizations; they may also have a large finance division and a scheduling section. All of these contribute to setting standards for output. You may be in a position to control or approve what literally hundreds of people control in larger industries. So you've got to be good, and you've got to do it with fewer people. Let's start with quality itself.

## DESCRIBING THE QUALITY YOU WANT SO YOU'LL GET RIGHT-ON RESULTS

What's good? Or, more important, what is best?

In defining store standards, Kirk Lowe took it slowly. Kirk was training a new manager, Bob McGee, for his Bed and Bath Shop.

Bob was inclined to be careless about store cleanliness. Store employees were to pick up paper, vacuum, restock stock and put pieces back in place. Kirk spoke to Bob about standards, but Bob didn't seem to improve. Kirk then set an example himself. In this way his manager gradually got the idea of cleanliness. Scolding didn't do it; example did. Example can be the best description.

In building something tangible, description is easy: "¼ inch thick," "two feet wide," "6 inches long." These measurements are easy to define, make and check. In software (paperwork or service) it may be ten times as hard to spell out your standards. What is acceptable quality in one of your assignments?

> The report you assign may include a definition of the problem, persons involved, and the solution recommended. These requirements themselves spell out part of the standards. You can then discuss requirements for defining the problem and how far the solution must go.

Bob Winslow made just such an assignment. He ordered an official report to be prepared by a consultant working for the Board of Education. It was labled "Manpower Planning Related to School Curriculum in the State." Sound rough? It was. Bob's criteria of acceptance (standard of quality) was:

1. Reflect the current plans and expenditures of 10 to 15 state and federal agencies.
2. Show industry's acceptance or rejection of school graduates.
3. Offer suggestions for improving the situation.

The consultant submitted a first draft. After looking at the rough copy, Bob said, "You don't have enough references here . . . your suggestion is not specific enough there," etc. In the next round, the report was accepted. It met his standards.

How do you want the finished assignment to look? Get the idea in your mind and describe it to the others involved or show them an example.

Any acceptable example of a completed assignment can quickly clarify your standards of quality. If there isn't any, pull out your best words and paint him a picture of what you want.

## HOW TO WEIGH THE TIME FACTOR FOR PROMPT ACTION

How long is enough? A person could be perfect if you let him work forever. But there's a break-even point after which you can't afford his time. Find this point.

Eddie Baker, manager of a supply warehouse, defined the steps and standards for one assignment to his supervisors: "Prepare and submit group activity report."

Step 1. Review all material received from assigned personnel.
   15 minutes is great. 30 minutes is O.K. 45 minutes is too long.
Step 2. Select items to be used and expand as necessary.
   1 hour . . . tops. 1½ hours . . . O.K. 2 hours . . . too long.
Step 3. Dictate to steno for review draft.
   15 minutes, great. 30 minutes, O.K. 45 minutes, too long.
Step 4. Review previous week's activity report for any follow-up items.
   5 minutes, tops. 10 minutes, O.K. 15 minutes, too long.
Step 5. Check arithmetic on work-in-process charts to be attached to report.
   5 minutes, tops. 10 minutes, O.K. 15 minutes, too long. (This assumes no major rework necessary.)
Step 6. Submit marked draft and chart to steno for typing. Upon completion review, sign and submit.
   5 minutes, tops. 10 minutes, O.K. 15 minutes, too long.
   Total time for this assignment: An hour and 45 minutes to three hours.

This is a minimum time. However, it gives Eddie and his supervisors a standard. Even if they don't make it, they know how far they are off and where to make improvements. Your man must know what his standard is. Maybe he can beat it or improve on it and save you time.

Reverting back to the previous standard—quality—Eddie says this report allows no misspelled words, bad grammar, typographical or mathematical errors, or omission of activity or event.

Other more general time standards are simply included in such statements as:

"It's due next Wednesday."
"Check with me Monday to see how far along you are."
"Allow two days to redo after Mrs. Johns sees it."
"Should take about two hours for the whole assignment."
"Let's review at 2 o'clock."

He should be able to allot *portions* of time:

Half of his time circulating among his people, half in administration.
Two-thirds of his time calling on customers, one-third in the office. Or
any division you choose.

Whether general or specific, you must weigh the time factor for
prompt action.

### SETTING THE PRICE YOU'LL PAY FOR
### SUCCESSFUL PERFORMANCE

Price can involve material or time.

It includes allowable rework, schedule, and many other variables.
Is meeting the schedule worth the price? Is a certain level of quality
worth the price? Will a less expensive material fill the bill? Will
prestige suffer? Will the recipient of the service suffer?

A shrewd manager balances the successful performance triangle:
Schedule—Quality—Budget. None should get the "short end of the
stick."

A part of the price may be the result of some of your own time
working with the man to make the assignment successful. This is
expensive, but it may set him up for future success.

If it's a buyer's market, you can set a price for an item and the seller
has to deliver regardless of what it costs to make it. Many companies
have gone bankrupt by not doing good work the first time and being
stuck with a set price. As a manager, you are a buyer of the work of
your own people. However, you also pay the bill for changes or
excessive rework. As you'll see in other chapters you're torn between
demanding satisfaction and having to pay the bill yourself.

I don't mean that you should always settle for less than the
best—but maybe you should on some occasions. Weigh it: is further
work worth the price?

John Kitchens is the stock supervisor in a production company and is in charge of ordering and storing materials. He ordered aluminum sheets cut in certain sizes. When the sheets arrived they were too short. The aluminum had been cut in a department of his company. Joe started to tell them that they should take it back because it was cut wrong, but he realized the cost involved. By consulting with the engineers he found it could be used in another area. Although he called up the cutting department and let them know about it, he actually saved the company money by readjusting. He also received a letter of thanks from the manager of the cutting department for taking the extra effort and avoiding the cost to them.

Your man must still learn to do things right. If it's possible to make him do it again and again for his own training, do it. He needs to be quality conscious, but don't pick up too large a tab for his practice. Set the standard of performance, then set the price you are willing to pay to make your man meet it.

## HOW TO MAKE ALLOWANCES FOR YOUR UNEXPLAINED STANDARDS

A man can follow your instructions, complete the assignment and still strike out. Why? He could meet your schedule, your quality, and your cost and still not have something right. There might be an abundance of unknown factors that he hasn't heard about.

—Tell him that you'd like to be invited to the meetings he will hold with purchasing and production.
—Tell him that you want a report of status several times before completion.
—Tell him you dislike "Joe Kernan in Purchasing" and would prefer he not listen to him.
—If he deals with the people in Scientific Computing or any other organization, tell him to leave them happy for the next time.
—Tell him to avoid stripping some other project in order to complete his own.
—Tell him if he can cut red tape, it's good but that he should leave sufficient records for the next guy.

These are the unknown factors!

These are some of the general standards of deportment. How is he expected to behave with the troops? How is he expected to leave other outfits he deals with? You want results, but you can't afford to have a Jack the Ripper or Lizzie Borden on your staff.

Therefore you've got to explain your unexplained standards.

Some managers hate the words "swell" and "lousy." One had better not put them in a report if that's the case. This is the X factor that drives an employee up the wall.

Unexplained standards are usually explained by example or after the fact. Make it easier on the other person and yourself by sitting down and digging out any of them that you can think of. Write down your personal whims and discuss them with any assignment. It may hurt your ego but it will help your man's performance.

Ron Munsky manages salesmen for a greeting card company. He told me that one standard he always forgets to mention until it happens is that he likes his instructions followed to the letter and in the order he recommends. If he says do "A, then B, then C," that's what he wants. I'd prefer that a man be left a little room to think and create, but not Ron. He penalizes a man that doesn't work in certain order. So in many cases his man wrestles with the unexplained. Be sure your employee doesn't.

## LETTING HIM HELP SET STANDARDS WILL
## BRING BETTER PERFORMANCE

If you let the other person help set up the job, the standards, or anything else, he's more likely to make it work. It becomes his idea. It is his and that's what is important in his world. His standards might even be better than yours.

Fred Sheffield, personnel director for a truck body company, related his experience with employee involvement in setting standards. He said that each time a new system is installed, production managers ask workers to improve on it. Each time a change is made in an assembly process, production managers check it with their people. So far, according to Fred, his men have made strong and appropriate requirements. On several occasions management has even had to lower some of their suggested standards as being too hard to meet. Put people in the act and they'll outdo themselves.

Even if he's lax in meeting a standard, the man will do better if he helps figure out the cure. Joe Lake, product manager in a busy final assembly department, had an employee whose quality was slipping. He handled all the wiring at a certain location on an item. Joe talked it over with an inspector and then brought the employee in and asked him how could "they" solve the problem. The employee immediately perked up, recommended solutions that mainly involved himself and showed improvement accordingly. He felt responsible for helping make the improvements work, and Joe now has a good quality record.

Ken Stricker discussed with Polly Malone, a keypunch operator, his intention to establish meaningful performance standards for her job. He needed this, he explained, in order to determine average, below average, and outstanding work. They then discussed how Ken would use the criteria to complete her semiannual employee review sheets. Polly now feels committed to making them work. Ken diplomatically got results in setting standards and getting commitment.

Commitment is the biggest part of the battle. Getting your employee to help set standards goes a long way toward getting him sold on turning out a better performance.

## HOW TO PREVENT USELESS WHEEL-SPINNING

A successful speaker once stated: "The best time to stop a talk is when you're through with the message." With a job as well, some people don't know when they're through.

Dave Cratchet, marketing manager in a production company, spelled it out this way: "When you have completed the project, drawn up the letter for me to sign and laid it on my desk, then you are through. Let me change or alter it if need be, but don't leave me to do the writing of the letter or the final draft of the plan. On the other hand, don't go on researching or coming up with other ideas if it is time to make the decision, write the letter and get it on the road."

Jeff Mendel holds a sales meeting every morning with each individual salesman for one hour and asks his plans and day's activities. Jeff is sales manager in a small company and has overreacted to the salesman's need for personal guidance. He is now wasting time in which the salesman should be seeing customers. He should check the salesman out, but isn't once a week, in depth, enough? He's caused all his salesman to join the wheel-spinning bunch.

Don Shoop is an old-time manager, retired to an administrative position in manufacturing. He is brilliant in figuring out what will and won't work. Don served on a committee along with eight other managers to plan safety promotion campaigns around the plant. Some of these men worked in lesser spots and really couldn't have cared less about the campaign. The chairman soon learned if a decision was needed on some expenditure or new promotional idea, he could get a clear answer from Don. He then got a rubber stamp answer from some of the others on the phone and went ahead with the plan. He eliminated all of the wheel spinning of convening the committee and trying to get group thinking, yet he had the fastest and best advice.

Wheel spinning takes many forms:

—Getting more information than needed to do the job.
—Checking with more people than necessary to get it done.
—Justifying minimum expenditures or moves.
—Unneeded reports.
—Unneeded committee meetings (from fear to act).
—Any other activity that doesn't materially help get the desired action.

The first opportunity that you have to check on your man, eliminate any superfluous reports, meetings, or other time-consuming activities that don't raise the quality of output proportionately.

## ASSURING THAT REQUIREMENTS ARE REALISTIC FOR THE ASSIGNMENT

Ron Munsky, the greetings card manager mentioned earlier, is extremely realistic. He has done the assignments and checked out people doing them until he has realistic expectations.

When he hires a new man he expects him to meet certain requirements in calling on stores. Each man has a territory with a number of stores. He is then given help to make a plan for covering a certain number in one day.

Ron figures that a man will take 11 minutes and a half on each store fixture. The average store has 5 units with 12 shelves and could have 99 to 108 items on each. He tells the man he'll have 1 hour and 45 minutes per store as a maximum and 1 hour 18 minutes as a minimum. This takes into consideration the area he'll cover, size of the store card department, driving time and store maintenance. Some stores won't require that much time; others will need more.

He expects the man to:

—eliminate out-of-stock conditions
—put in cards with envelopes
—interleaf instead of putting behind
—eliminate duplication on display.

He has watched his men enough and has also done the work himself so that he knows the requirements are right. It is easy to expect too many stores, too large an area, or too many functions within each store to be covered. Ron's company sends him men to train because the management knows he'll do it right.

If it's unrealistic you must take the blame for his failure and you both want to succeed. So look closely at an assignment to see that it is possible for the man to do what you want.

## DETERMINING THAT THE STANDARDS ARE WITHIN RANGE OF HIS CAPABILITIES

The standards could be good ones—but not for the individual. If so, you're still in trouble. Let's make them right for him.

Kirk Lowe, the Bed and Bath Shop owner, has a manager looking after it for him. He wishes this manager could control the bookkeeping, use discretion in ordering stock and really charm customers. But he can't; he's not that type. All he can do is ring up sales, take the money, and keep shop. Kirk doesn't like it, but that is the way that it is. He can accept the man for what he is and let him operate within his capabilities, change managers, or he can set up a long-range program and try to enhance his abilities. Meanwhile, he shouldn't lose sleep because of what he can't do.

You have to know your men; there is no substitute for this knowledge.

If you know that a man'a ability to sell an idea is nil . . . it is useless to require that he meet with another and sell him, unless you are willing to pay some penalty for the training time. It's like asking a color-blind man to coordinate your decorating scheme. It's just not within his range.

Joe Blake is a shrewd training manager in a telephone company. He would not dare send Argo Smith, his technical training supervisor, to see a manager about planning training because he knows that while Argo can do the training, he can't negotiate. He sends Rich Phillips to do the negotiating. Joe has even sent them both when he felt the terminology may be above one's head and the diplomacy above the other's. This may sound like duplication, but he's got his men figured to a "T" and won't let either one take on a job outside his abilities. He's trying to improve the skills of both, but meanwhile he's using the capabilities of each. This is one trait that helps give him a reputation as a brilliant manager in the telephone company.

Ask yourself about an employee: Has he had any previous experience in the line? Was he successful? If his mechanical aptitude is low, then expect low performance when he has to deal with mechanics. This is why it is beneficial to go over both the assignment and the man's capabilities before trying to match them. You can then be sure they are within his range.

## LOOKING AT YOUR REQUIREMENTS THROUGH HIS EYES IN ORDER TO PRODUCE WORKABLE STANDARDS

The man doing the work might see the whole assignment as a drag while you think it's great fun!

Each year the Air Force sends three or four men to spend nine months studying purchasing and production in an aircraft manufacturing company. Jim Royal, manager of public relations, handles their trip and their program while in the plant. Jim called Ray Stone in and delegated the assignment. He also gave Ray a free hand. Much to Jim's horror the assignment went downhill and he found the men missing appointments and needing help with outside arrangements. When Jim sat down to talk it over with Ray, he discovered the problem. Instead of seeing the job as a worthwhile assignment, Ray felt like it had been passed off on him. He detested it, and thus he did little to make it work. Only after Jim explained its whole scope and challenged him did Ray pick up the planning and make it meaningful. When Jim looked at it from Ray's eyes he saw the problem. He was smart enough to get it corrected and get a letter of gratitude from the Air Force for a good program.

"Why should a person want to do it my way?" is a good question for the astute manager to ask himself before making an assignment. Either he respects your title, experience, or personality, or he has another reason. If you were in his shoes would you want to do it that way?

Charles Evans, the office service manager says, "He's running his own department. I want him to make his own decisions and use his own style."

Ron Munsky, the greeting card sales manager, says, "I want things done my way—so he must learn my way."

Your man needs to know which way it will be—yours or his. Is some part of the assignment unreasonable in his eyes? Be sure you clear it up. Why are you doing it a certain way?

Does "light blue" mean the same to you and him? Does large size mean the same? Are you on the same wave length with the words and definitions?

A newspaper woman called on Joe Blaine, manager of a dress shop. Her purpose was to put together the advertising for ten stores who had reserved the whole middle section of the paper. Joe was to be the coordinator. Joe said, "I wanted everything together and ready to run the following Wednesday." On Monday he checked with her, "Where's the ad?" He found that several of the stores had not yet turned in their ads. He got nervous, and with the newspaper woman, went to the stores and reminded the owners of their ads. They had expected the woman to push them to meet the deadline. She had expected them to come through with the finished ads. In her eyes the requirements were different. Joe couldn't very well get upset when he had not made his requirements clear.

Take a close look at the assignment as your man sees it and you can get your standards on the same track with his thinking.

## CHECKING HIS UNDERSTANDING OF STANDARDS
## BEFORE PUTTING HIM ON HIS OWN

Jeff Mendel counsels his salesmen, "When a prospect comes forth with an objection, repeat it back to him. This assures that you know what he is talking about." The same applies in checking out an assignment. Let the man repeat it back to you and you can determine whether or not his interpretation is the same as yours.

In getting his new store set up, John Law specified pegboard walls. The walls were already finished with plasterboard and the pegboard had to be framed in on top. John had seen other such jobs fail and intended to have this one right. He specified cross bracing along the top and bottom so that the board would not undulate. He insisted on good quality board large enough to fit quarter-inch brackets without paint cracking. He then had the carpenter repeat his specifications back to him, and finally, he wrote some of them down. He was pleased because the job was just what he wanted. John's checking on the contractor resulted in successful work.

Alice Mars, formerly manager of a business college, asked Jane Rolls to stamp some envelopes while she was teaching a class. Jane picked up the envelopes and proceeded to do just that. They were stamped, sealed and ready to be mailed when Alice came out of class—except that she had intended that they go unsealed for less expensive postage rate. Alice just didn't realize that Jane didn't know this. She should have checked Jane's understanding and saved money on postage and temper.

Be safe—let a man review with you before turning him loose.

## FIXING THE POINT AT WHICH YOU'LL TAKE
## A READING ON HIS MEETING STANDARDS

How long will the assignment take?
How experienced is he?
How much money is invested? Goodwill? Etc.

These are the kinds of questions that help you determine how soon you need to assess your man's performance. There is a whole chapter later in the book devoted to building in checkpoints, but it is important to take a quick look at the subject while we're discussing performance standards.

Jerry Jasper was asked to teach a course in a vocational-technical school. He had been teaching for 12 years and knew how to do it. Jerry planned his course, ordered supplies, reserved the room and completed all of the other necessary arrangements. He was pleased to get a call from Lee Mathison, the manager of instruction. "Tell me your plans," Lee asked and after hearing, he agreed with Jerry that everything sounded right.

But on the night of the third class, Jerry looked up and was astonished to see Lee walk in and take a seat on the back row. He sat through the whole class and came up later and said, "Congratulations, Jerry, the class was fine." Lee's purpose was to watch the class and the instructor to see that the training met the vocational school's standards. He took a reading early enough to see that the students got the best. Lee was later promoted to assistant director for the school partly because of his keen and timely interest in instruction.

Plan to do the same when you make an assignment. Fix a point at which you'll check up to see that his standards coincide with what you have in mind. It can save time and money in the long run and keep you the title of action-getter.

## HOW TO AVOID GENERAL STANDARDS AND SHOOT FOR SPECIFIC RESULTS

You want the job done right. It's hard for the other fellow to know what right is. When a job is finished, you can look at it and tell him it's okay, but can he repeat the process and come up with an okay every time?

Probably not, if he doesn't know what added up to a correct tally in the first place. You'll have to help him get the same correct results each time.

The section manager for Manufacturing Engineering in a production company is Eldred Mann. He often helps his management in the preparation of memos to other departments and companies. Eldred decided that it was time to train someone else to help with this responsibility and chose Ed Stokely. Ed was excited about this opportunity and really dived into it. When he delivered the first draft of a letter to be signed by Mr. Mayner, Eldred sat him down and went over the whole thing to help him in future work. "Mr. Mayner likes all big words eliminated. He likes short sentences and very personal feeling in his writing." Ed reworked the letter along those lines and came up with a winner. After a few more letters, Eldred has been able to turn all of the letter writing over to Ed and take on other management duties. He specifically showed him how he could get consistent results.

Suppose you are managing a supermarket and direct your attention to the product displays. When you hire a man and train him, you tell him that you expect the displays completed by 9:25. The store opens at 9:30. You expect all paraphernalia such as boxes, excelsior, wrappings and twines and ropes to be out of the area then, and all damaged produce removed. The round produce should be lined up and stacked in rows. Prices should be displayed below each rack. If a price has changed upward, a fresh sticker should be put on rather than a mark-through . . . and so on.

Tell a man specifically when you want the completed work, how much time he will be allowed to spend to accomplish this, and how he will know his work is of good quality each time he finishes it.

## ESTABLISHING ANY ALLOWABLE TRADE-OFFS BETWEEN QUALITY AND COST

Jim Shannan serves as Warrantee Committee Manager in a manufacturing organization and has to think fast and correctly. A designer told him: "The part will work better if the handle is moved to the other side." Jim thought: in the process of moving, a bulkhead would also have to be moved and the part really works pretty well as it is. It would be an expensive move and would not make that much difference. His decision was to leave it as it is.

Jim has become the warrantee committee manager because he knows how to weigh and make trade-offs between cost and quality, or, as in this example, how to take no action at all. He balances economy and quality.

You must be able to ask yourself how much more effective the next expenditure will make the project. Sometimes it pays to do nothing, but only after weighing cost and quality.

The cover of a set of manuals had been laid out well. It had been reviewed by several concerned individuals and given the go-ahead. Then just as it was ready for the production process, another manager saw it and said, "It'll look better with a second person shown on the cover." The whole project was redone at additional cost and as a result, ran over budget. Was that change really necessary?

On the other hand, a salesman presented several potential awards to John Thompson, a Quality Motivation Manager, for use as recognition. The pins ranged from $5 to $15 in price. Over the year, the awards could be given to as many as 500 people out of the 32,000 in the company. Several managers recommended the higher-priced item: "Nothing is too good for our people." However, John held his ground . . . that the designs were basically the same and either would do. He bought a lower-priced item and over a three-year period got nothing but compliments. His trade-off ability later lead to a promotion in Employee Relations.

The ability to trade off is a byproduct of experience. Start now to analyze how much you can afford to rework or redo to get quality, then let your men in on your thinking.

## DECIDING THE "QUALITY OR SCHEDULE" PRIORITY

One of your major jobs is maintaining the delicate balance between quality and schedule. You control the balance and must set the priorities. Bill Williams came up through Master Scheduling and controls schedules and set-up time. Recently he had a fixture built and installed. In the process he saw that parts brought in from an outside source were not as good as they ought to be. He had a choice of sending them back and getting new ones, or using them and getting the fixture installed on time. Since five departments were waiting for the fixture he analyzed the pros and cons. He called the outside company and said he'd keep the parts at a reduced price and went ahead and put them in. All of the managers commended him for not holding up their production schedule, plus the fact that he won other praises for saving some money. He had merely assessed correctly the quality/schedule priority, and he came out looking wonderful. You must be ready to do the same.

Once when a major aircraft system was delivered, millions were spent to make the delivery date. A penalty was imposed for every day that the craft was late. This really inspired the team to break their backs to make delivery. But the rush placed on every part and process caused a premium price to be paid, supplies to incur higher costs and quality to be forgotten. If there had been a national emergency this sort of rush might have been justified, but not to meet a paper date.

A man must learn to appreciate time and schedules. Make him toe the line, but don't throw quality out the window in the process. In the previous example, rework literally skyrocketed because the push to make schedule caused many errors.

Some managers stress quality—each item must be perfect. Others are just as hung on a schedule. The two have got to balance, unless a customer or outside force dictates otherwise. As an action-getter you must be able to balance factors as well as a performer in the circus.

## INSISTING ON REWORK UNTIL YOUR STANDARDS ARE MET SUCCESSFULLY

Your man's going to be better off in the long run if you teach him high standards. If it means doing a job over and over, it'll help him get the message to do it right the first time (provided you're not paying a premium for his lessons in rework).

Any work that comes into your organization or from another company should be correct. I don't believe in showing mercy when it comes to getting what I pay for. If I pay for good work, then I want it and I don't mind asking for it again and again until I get it. This might help the other organization to realize a need to give the best service —in the beginning.

Don Bynam, a supplier for a Craft Shop, delivered several dozen wooden plaques. These were used for decoupage and were selling at a good rate. In checking them out after a couple of weeks, Allen Gonsalves, the manager, discovered that the wood was warping slightly. Allen called Don and asked that they be replaced. They were. In a couple of weeks the same thing happened. Allen had them replaced a second time. The outcome? Don decided they should be made from a different kind of wood in the first place. He changed his wood and there has been no trouble since. Allen got first rate wood for his customers and Don eliminated a problem of his own. Neither would have happened if Allen had not asked him to do and redo. Customers come back to Allen's shop because they know he'll have the best quality supplies. He persists until he gets it.

Insist on rework to meet your standards and benefit yourself and others.

You've looked at standards from every angle. As an action-getter you must be able to set the standards and see that they are met.

Review for a moment the vital aspects of doing this:

—Learn to balance Quality-Cost-Schedule plus the unknown.
—Assure that standards are realistic and within a person's capabilities.
—Let him help set them or correct them.
—Check his understanding before turning him loose.
—Get it done over for the benefit of all concerned.

Now that you've got your standards set to guarantee a successful performance, let's turn our attention to picking the right person.

# 5

## HOW TO ASSIGN THE RIGHT PERSON
## AND LESSEN YOUR MANAGERIAL LOAD

Let's see how we can take some of the weight off of our backs by giving part of the work to someone else—the right man.

Work is assigned on many bases: to the man who works fast, works well, gives accurate and complete work, according to interests, for broadening and development, and in many cases just because a man's handy or he's the last resort. You want to get action—the right kind and on time—so let's look at how we can beat the average or the ordinary.

—Look closely at the man's strength and weaknesses
—Make the assignment match his talent
—Get out of his hair and let him do it his way if possible
—Let him know who to turn to if he needs help

Start with the man and what you know about him.

### HOW TO DISCOVER EACH MAN'S STRENGTH
### AND WEAKNESS SO YOU CAN PICK A WINNER

One day I was helping my secretary with some routine stuffing and mailing. I was in a separate room and ran out of item A. I sat and pondered how to get her to bring me a fresh supply without her feeling that she was waiting on me. Then the light dawned. "Hey, I know something you don't," I declared. And then I counted to ten and said (just as she was rounding the corner), "On your way in here please bring me a handful of item A." That's a dirty trick and I only use it to make a point. Nothing beats knowing the person you're dealing with. Certainly if you're giving him work to do, you need to know him to assure that he can do what you expect. You know how to use his strengths and avoid his weaknesses and, in the process, get action.

Charles Evans does this. He manages an office services department, buying, stocking, and dispersing supplies to other departments in the company. Recently he had a new man, Doug Carlisle, that needed assigning. The front desk that handled outside orders was empty, due to a vacationing employee, so Charles decided to let Doug try it. In short order, he discovered that Doug didn't like to push vendors and readily accepted excuses from them. He tried helping him with the job but soon learned that his whole personality resisted push. Knowing that someone strong on dealing with people was needed in the job, Charles decided to try Doug in a new spot. Charles put him in the internal records section and he has thrived. He turned a potential loser into a winner by testing him for strengths and weaknesses, then using his strength. Charles has earned the reputation of knowing how to handle people. You don't have to use a whole job for a test fit. You could use a short or simple task to get a reading on your man.

Joe Tanner did it the easy way. Joe runs a clothing store and needed part time help. Hiring someone is often an uncertain proposition. Joe told Beth Stanfield to come in and work several hours for several days part time just to get the feel of things after she had called and asked if he needed help. He told her he wasn't making a definite decision; that he was trying several prospects. He watched the way she handled customers, learned stock and tried to keep busy. At the end of the time, he was pleased with Beth. She's a regular in his store now.

In determining a man's abilities as a winner, consider such points as:

—Does he have a sense of timing? Can he get people to take action and still like him?

—Can he put together a total project and account for each part?
—Can he follow instructions?

## MAKING THE ASSIGNMENT TALLY
## WITH HIS TALENT

Roy Threlkil is president of a merchants association and has to use the other managers according to their abilities. In a meeting once, he asked Jan, "How about formulating the rules and regulations for our prize contest?" Jan agreed. Roy really meant for him to get everything ready so the merchants could accept or reject it. Jan went further and planned newspaper ads and promotion. They were abominable. Roy took one look and decided the man was out of his range. In the next meeting he asked Pat Giles to handle just the advertising. Pat draws fairly well and had done layout work. Pat succeeded. Even Jan liked Pat's layout, and so did the other merchants. The result: Roy received praises for a successful contest, thanks to getting the right assignments in line with the right talents. The old story about the square peg in a round hole is still true.

Clyde was an irascible, pessimistic, phlegmatic employee in a manufacturing company. Clyde's boss, Mark Doughty, was shrewd. He managed over 700 people in Quality Control and Air Force Liaison. One function was to put out charts, figures and statistics to keep the rest of the company and the Air Force informed. Clyde's strong point was making charts. He also thrived on statistics. Mark takes advantage of Clyde's long suit. Whenever he needs any budgeting or charting of performance or other reporting that can be relegated to statistical charts, he turns to Clyde. Mark has never yet gone into a major budget meeting without coming out smelling like a rose. Clyde keeps him looking good and Mark keeps Clyde on the right assignments.

There is a difference between talents and capabilities. Talent refers to specialty and ability that one person has and another may not have. Capability defines the degree or amount of that talent. A little looking will tell you the man's likes and dislikes. Closer observation will tell you where his talent lies. Once you find that a man has a talent, give him a try with it and see how his capability rates. Make his work area correspond and you've got a winner.

## HOW TO LET HIM DO IT HIS WAY
## AND STILL MEET YOUR STANDARDS

Ron Munsky in Chapter 2 had to have things done his way regardless of whether the guy could meet his standards or not. Lacking any information on past performance or reason to judge differently you may feel the same. After you've studied your man's past work and know him, he is probably much better off when allowed to choose his own way.

Bob Hill trained Elaine Carson to be the new manager for his textile store. She has very good color sense, can keep books, can coordinate items of purchase as to quality of colors and is aware of costs. Early in her training Bob said, "Elaine, pick out the towels you like." She selected like a veteran. He then said, "Elaine, choose the boxes and wrapping paper that you prefer." He watched as she did that. Little by little he has seen that Elaine meets his high standards and yet he hasn't told her to make any particular choice. He has turned the purchasing over to her entirely and she is doing it just as well as he could and she feels like it is her store. She is enthusiastic and sells the shop at every conversation. Bob has obtained a fine manager by letting her do things her way.

As quickly as you see that a man is on your track let him pursue his own style. He'll give you more than you expect. Bernie Elliott, a product assurance manager in a milling plant, knows how to give a man rein. If he wants a letter written to a fellow product assurance manager in California, and the subject is the calibration laboratory, he calls Charlie Grace. Charlie supervises Bernie's lab and knows everything there that's worth knowing about instrument calibration. Bernie states briefly, "Charlie, I need a letter to Mel Swenson in California. He needs to know about our latest equipment because he is interested in some of his own. Can you do it for me by Thursday?" Charlie delivers the goods and is authoritative. Bernie has the privilege of handing it to his secretary as is or adding any casual comment at the beginning or end. He allows Charlie to discuss the lab his way and in turn satisfy Bernie's requirements. Mel thinks Bernie is the smartest man around on the subject of calibration and Charlie Grace thinks Bernie's smart for listening to him.

—Let the other person know your standards carefully.

—Check him to see that he understands.

—See if he wishes to do it differently; if his method is logical, let him try it.

—Check in along the way to see that he's on target and then let him go.

Capitalize on his brain power by letting it be a part of the project, only check to see that he is going to get your results in the long run.

## LEARNING BOTH MEANINGS OF "COMPROMISE"

Compromise means to give in and accept or do less than your principles say you should.

Compromise means to give in a little in order to meet someone part way, without selling your principles short.

The first meaning is a bad one. Let's forget about it. The second is a legitimate one that makes good management sense. The Chinese say the bamboo reed bends with the wind while the staunch oak breaks. Compromise keeps you from breaking—you bend a little to get results.

There's the compromise between schedule and quality to keep one from breaking your back while getting the other.

There's the compromise between cost and quality which allows you to trade off at the most favorable point.

There's the compromise between cost and schedule which defines the stopping point.

You've already looked at these three and seen how to maintain a happy balance. Compromise in its best sense is the answer. There's the compromise between your expressed standards and performance. (Remember: the definition says giving a little without selling your principles.)

—You asked for the work to be double spaced and put in a notebook.

The secretary put it in the notebook, but it was single spaced. It is still usable, so why make her do it over? Let her know that she has missed your standards. You accept it this time, but you won't next time.

You asked the Data Processing supervisor to give you a print-out that shows every development course your supervisors have had. He states he won't do that because Management Selection has just had the same thing done. Look at theirs and see if it'll do for you. If so, it'll save your company money.

In short, be willing to make trade-offs in order to get the best over-all job done. This takes discretion and just plain guts. But then isn't the successful manager 50 percent intelligence and 50 percent guts?

## HOW TO LOOK SMART AND STAY OUT OF HIS WAY

You set the standards.

You really need to check on them, but not *too* often! Don't breathe down your man's neck and handicap the whole operation. If he's brand new, then you'll check a little closer, but if he's experienced, give him freedom. After all, you hired him for a certain talent. Let him use it.

In an annual management meeting in a huge production company, Jim Handley turned over arrangements and facilities to Joe George, who had done similar work with great success many times in the past. Joe was the essence of dependability. Jim turned over promotion and publicity to Charles Emerson, who had an excellent record in that field.

A couple of weeks before the meeting, Al, one of the officers in the organization, started worrying. He stated, "I don't know where we will plug in the microphones in the auditorium." Jim told him, "Don't sweat it; Joe knows exactly where and he is the one responsible." Later Al was seen trying to tell the publicity man how to write the flyer. Again Jim told him, "Lay off; Charles knows everything that's needed in order to put out the best flyer. Just leave him alone and let him do it." Everything worked out smoothly. Jim Handley just made the assignments while the other men delivered an excellent meeting. Jim later received an award of merit for the excellence of the meetings.

Delegate to capable people, then let them do their jobs. Don't bother them about the details.

There, follow-up is one thing but unnecessary harassment is another. If a man knows what he is doing and you know he knows what he is doing, let him alone. That's delegation. You'll end up looking better.

## SPLITTING UP AN ASSIGNMENT SO YOU CAN USE THE BEST OF SEVERAL PEOPLE

Jim Handley had a big assignment to parcel out. Rather than expecting one man to deliver the whole annual meeting, he broke it up into specialized parts and put specialists on each one. People raved about the smoothness of the meeting and Jim was the hit of the day. He split the responsibility to get the best.

Bob Harrison, a training manager, is a master at splitting assignments. He really pulls out the best in each man. He put Frank in charge of a project developing a new visual aid machine. Bob knows that Frank's inventiveness and eagerness to try something new is his biggest asset: he will experiment until he finds a better way of doing something. He'll also splice new information into the old format. Frank was a good choice for the project, but he had one stumbling point: he couldn't care less about time. Bob in many previous projects had never been able to make this man schedule conscious. This project had to make the date. Since one of his men, Anson Lynde, was acting as Sales Manager for the project, Bob merely said, "Anson, the machine has to be delivered on June 3; you are responsible for that." So Anson kept a keen eye on the time. He kept at Frank to make the due date. The best of two people made a successful project.

You may sit and wish that each of your people be well rounded and brilliant in all areas. Let's face it: They aren't and you probably don't have money nor time to make it happen. So capitilize on what they do have. Use their best talents and let them be successful. The better they look, the better you look.

## ALLOWING THE MAN TIME TO LEARN AND STRENGTHEN HIS PERFORMANCE

Perhaps instead of a book called "Get Action," we ought to have a book called "Get Responsibility," because it seems that one of the main keys to action lies in the individual's feeling of responsibility.

My wife, Mary, taught a class of youngsters in the Primary Department of Sunday School. These little fellows had pictures they were ready to paste on the cover of a booklet they were making. One very proudly pasted on the picture, and as Mary watched him, she realized that he was pasting it on crooked. The decision had to be made whether to leave him alone and tell him, "You're working nicely," or to say, "That's crooked, let's straighten it." Which was more important? A straight picture or the fact that this youngster had a chance to do it himself and be completely responsible for the final product? I wonder if in industry we're not guilty of causing the individual to react exactly the way we tell him to. He has no creative originality because he has no responsibility. Can we not set up a requirement that allows him to do things in his own style so that he feels a part of the work? Allow the individual to learn and feel responsible.

A crowd descended on the registration desk at a convention just as it opened. Three or four convention members acting as clerks were casting around trying to set up a procedure. As Sam Devon, one of the other managers, and I stood and watched, we grew concerned that they needed help. I started over to see if I could help, when Sam said, "Hold it, just wait a minute. If you and I go over there, we'll add two more to the confusion. They have considered this ahead of time and should work it out in a few minutes if we leave them alone." Sam was right. In short order the system began working and the confusion abated. The sign-up went as it should. Allow your man time for learning and keep on the sidelines until he learns. In the process he will gain confidence and give you a good performance.

## SHOW HIM HOW HE FIGURES IN THE
## TOTAL SETUP

The sooner your man learns the whole setup the sooner he's eligible for a bigger job. He ought to be anxious to learn for that reason. He'll be better able to perform his own job if he's got the whole perspective, so tie him to the larger picture.

Here's the way Jack Moses, a successful statistics manager, did it.

An employee, new to the department, asked how to use the standard pricing data in preparing a cost proposal. Realizing the importance of using this data properly and that this employee had a reputation for being most conscientious in his previous work assignment, I took the time to "walk through" all the data, not just the small area he was questioning at that time.

He was very appreciative and while he has not had occasion to use all the data in the preparation of a proposal, I am confident he understands the whole and uses the parts better.

You don't even need to wait for him to say "help." Do it anyway. I found long ago that if I could describe the total picture to my secretary, she could see that a particular letter or report fitted in exactly. It gives the person a little more to draw on, in case your specific instructions haven't hit the mark. It's insurance for action.

## DECIDING WHETHER ANYONE WILL RUN INTERFERENCE FOR HIM

Can he handle the public relations angle? Sell? Account? Negotiate? Schedule? Advertise?

According to the project, he may need a front man to clear a path for him.

Dick Stein created a smart quality assurance program and installed it in a company. It involved all departments and created a method of setting standards and gauging performance. He selected Al Means to initiate and run the program. Over a year and a half the program was extremely successful and rework cost dropped tremendously.

Dick had helped Al become an authority in this type of program and with visitors coming in from all over the country, Al knew what was going on everywhere. Dick decided the program should be sold to the Air Force and he decided to send Al to explain it. But he knew Al would need help in selling it, particularly with the details of marketing and in dealing with the military. He turned to the marketing department and picked George Kalendar, a good salesman to accompany Al. They made a good team. George ran interference and explained to the military what they could and could not do, and Al explained the program. Dick got his sale because he put in the right team.

If your man is handling a critical project and needs someone to break a trail, give him someone. It can be the boost that makes for a successful performance.

## MAKING SURE HE WILL TAKE YOUR OPINIONS AS SUGGESTIONS AND NOT SHAKE IN HIS BOOTS

Some people jump when the boss says jump. Some bosses like to act like God. There's a time to jump and a time to play God. But your employees are being paid to think too, so let's hope they've got enough sense to stand up for what they believe. I've seen men take every little whisper that the boss makes as seriously as orders and then institute change. A man's got to be able to weigh the opinions you give and decide whether it's a nice-to-know comment or a request for action. Help him make the distinction. Deliver me from the man who quakes in his boots every time the boss breathes. Help him understand whether or not he must react with your every statement.

Bill Martin, an administrative supervisor in a printing plant, arrived at his own successful ways for reading the boss.

Depending on the disposition of the boss, a statement that says, "I think it would look better in red" can be an opinion or a suggestion to change. Bill checks him out by saying, "Yes, you may be right. However unless you want it changed, I think we'll leave it in yellow."

The boss may say, "I wish the wood were a little darker." Bill tries, "Yes, it just didn't turn out very dark."

If the boss says, "I'd like to paint the door on the side," he can be checked by saying, "It doesn't look like this plan will allow that."

Check-out statements enable you to see if he's ordering or observing. Of course, if it is an order and Bill's already expressed contrary opinion, then Bill says, "Yes, sir," and quickly.

Keep these pointers in mind and help your employees take your suggestions without blindly jumping.

## DETERMINING THE NUMBER OF STRIKES BEFORE HE IS OUT

You've set standards, picked your man, and told him all about the standards. You're sure he's ready. How liberal are you? Will you allow him to strike out a time or two before he's out? Will you let him be wrong? Is the project so critical that it must be right the first time at all costs? Determine how many strikes he can take.

Dan was given the chance to supervise. The boss, Bob James, manager of Sales Promotion Section, gave him time, and unfortunately Dan botched it. Dan had 12 men who developed visual aids and operating procedures for showing products. Dan took total responsibility. He knew the products, but he didn't know people—he couldn't give clear instructions or handle people without irritating them.

Bob sat down with him and called attention to his difficulties. He suggested that Dan ought to handle Maggie Windom carefully since she was very sensitive; that he ask Dave Clarke's advice on building one of the projects since Dave was really proud of his ability. Bob James advised him how to handle each member of the group. He also advised Dan that he had one more chance. Dan took another crack at it and succeeded in short order, thanks to Bob's help. Bob has made another successful supervisor and is now grooming Dan to take his place so he can move on up the line.

We can learn from a successful manager like Bob, not only how to give a man help, but also how to let him know how many strikes before he is out. He should be told if this is his final chance.

In the same Sales Promotion outfit, Jerry Konger was assigned to mockups. He developed two that weren't right and had to be redone by someone else. Bob tried to discover if there was anything he could do to help Jerry correct his mistakes. He then told Jerry, "We can't afford the rework. If the next aren't right, we'll have to try you at something else." Jerry knew he had better bear down and get them right. He did. You must follow along the same lines although it sometimes seems heartless. Let your man know how many strikes he has before he is out.

## MAKING SURE HE KNOWS WHOSE EAR TO BEND
## IF HE NEEDS HELP

You're responsible—you made the assignment. However, many people helped you prepare it. You could answer most of the questions about it, but there are others who could also help your man. Is there another authority that he could contact if he needs help? Is there an expert or specialist that could give him more information than you can?

Claude Peak, foreman in a metal bonding department, has this down to an art. When he assigned a project to Dave, he also gave Dave some advice: "If it's a problem with sealing the part, call Yeader at extension 2964. If there's any shortage of small parts, call Scott at 3927. If you have trouble interpreting the manufacturing procedures, call Derick at 3842." Older hands know who to call for advice, but a new man may need to be steered in the right direction. Claude seldom has trouble telling his men where to turn for assistance. Because his men are well guided, others don't mind helping them. In this way Claude maintains a smooth work flow from his department.

If there are others that can lighten the load for you, find out who they are. They may be able to help one of your people better and more quickly than you can—and you'll still get credit for being the smart one who knows how to delegate effectively.

## HOW TO ASSIGN WORK TO THE MAN WHO DOESN'T REPORT TO YOU

Even if you don't have line authority flowing in the right direction for you, you can sometimes compensate in other ways. A little selling, recognition, challenge, or other quality will help you get a man to eagerly do the job for you.

Van Clifton works closely with Joe Baine, regional supervisor of a large restaurant association. Van manages food services in a factory where Joe's company furnishes the food. Van is a shrewd man who realizes that while he has no direct supervision over Joe, he nevertheless must get Joe to do certain things.

Van studied the supervisor carefully and learned his strengths and weaknesses so that he knows how to deal with him successfully. Van told me in an interview, "Joe wears his feelings on his sleeve and they get in the way of his thinking. I try to look at the food service problem from his standpoint."

"I asked for a production chart on a new kitchen after the bakery was completed. He questioned why I wanted a chart approved by the

Health Department when the department had approved the building plans. I showed him that the restaurant association's request for new refrigerator, freezer and storage space would change the floor space, making new approval necessary. When he realized that the new space would benefit his organization, he became very cooperative. This was only one example of the necessity of handling him carefully. By doing this I can always get results with him." This probably accounts for Van's promotion to coordinator of services in the Employee Relations Division.

Bill Dixon is group supervisor in a Data Processing organization. He outlines his action-getting requirements like this: "The girl who types for me is another man's secretary. Sometimes it takes some effort to keep her from feeling put upon—that's how it is now. However, I have observed her admiration for baseball teams, the Braves in particular. Lo and behold, a typing request proceeded by a comment on Hank Aaron's batting record or Phil Niekro's knuckle ball produce results far beyond any appeals to relative priorities or my requirements. I can get my typing done quicker than some of the men with full time secretaries. I've just learned how to appeal to her."

Let's learn from Van's and Dick's experience and appeal to the other person for action without necessarily having to rely on authority.

—Take a little extra time to share an interest.
—Take a little extra time to understand his motivation.
—In other words, take time to talk in his terms and you get action from him.

## HOW TO SWAP WORKERS PRONTO IF THE SELECTION WON'T WORK

If it won't work, change it. Save time, your worker's feelings, and his face. One reason for keeping track of his progress is to change his assignment if he's not going to make it when the assignment is due. It can be done without making him look bad.

Bonnell Craven, manager of the craft shop mentioned earlier, discovered that her new teacher wasn't demonstrating enough of the technique in a decoupage class. So she eased in and helped with the next session. She discovered that the teacher's problem was mainly a lack of motivation. Bonnell continued to stay with her and see that things were covered. When the next class was formed, Bonnell said she was teaching it herself and later got another teacher. When she discovered the lack of motivation she felt it was futile to try to develop the teacher further. She just wasn't right for the job. The next step was to see that neither the students nor the teacher suffered. Later she got a teacher who worked well. The students praised Bonnell's efforts.

Be sweet; be charming; but accomplish something too. The obligation is to get the job done. So try to spare feelings and use diplomacy, but above all else get someone else on the job in time, if necessary.

## HOW TO USE A "STRAW BOSS" AND STILL MANAGE SUCCESSFULLY

A "straw boss" can pull it all together. He's not really the manager, but the manager has asked him to look after things. In other words, without turning the job loose, the manager can look to one man to keep an eye on several people's work. It's not a strong arrangement, but it beats looking after a group of individuals. It also gives a man a chance to prove himself.

You're going to put together a proposal for manufacturing a product and submit it to a company. You ask John Dickenson to handle the R.F.Q. (request for quotations) meeting. People from Finance, Scheduling, Computing, Engineering and several affected areas are present. They're responsible operators in their own fields, but for this operation, someone has to organize them in order to put a quotation together in time. Since you've got many other time-consuming duties, John's the straw boss. If you need to know about the meeting's progress, ask John If someone's slow, John pushes.

You've asked Jay Williams and three others to develop a plan for evaluating engineering output. You're interested in their research, preliminary work and schedule commitment, so you tell the four to analyze what's being done. You say, "Jay, you look after it." He's straw boss. It's the simplest and most informal form of delegation.

My wife does it without realizing it. She sends three kids out to work in the yard. She tells each to take a section to weed, but she tells Susan, "You see that they do it."

Pick a capable man and try him out with this informal means of delegation. Let him be the "straw boss" thus keeping control in your hands and giving you only one man to ask questions of. This also gives him a chance to show you what he can do.

Whom will you pick to lessen your managerial load? Let's take another look at the critical questions you must ask if you're to pick the right person.

—Does he tell others what to do? Can he give informal advice?
—Is he concerned about finishing a job?
—Does he ask questions about other jobs? Is he interested in all the work?
—Can he check up the line with ease?
—Does he have real self-confidence?
—Can he take corrections? Can he make corrections without arousing offense?
—Can he transmit instructions effectively?
—Does he have a sense of priority and timing?
—Is he responsible with materials and expenses?

If he fills the majority of these questions with a yes answer, give him the job. You can almost stop your worrying, because you've got a winner. Next, help him set your job high on his priority list.

# 6

## PUTTING YOUR JOB HIGH ON HIS PRIORITY LIST TO GET TIMELY ACTION

A man has to know what comes first—which job is the most important—because of the end results required, or because a job has to be done sequentially before another can fall into place. This is not only a matter of scheduling but also of his attitude as to where priorities lie.

Take Walter Young, who has a series of jobs coming to him from various organizations.

—He's a busy man who has to stay on his toes.
—Can he let one job go to do another?
—Should he satisfy one man and let another wait?
—Job X came in on January 1 and Job Y came in on January 3, yet pressure is on to get out Job Y first. Should he?
—Job W is going to move straight through; Job Z will have to have some preliminary work done in order to get it out on time; should he go ahead and start Z?
—One man is easy to get along with but another isn't. There's a decision coming as to whose job is done next. Should he let the nice guy wait?

As an action-getting manager, what'll you do to get your job on time? Let's examine the factors and the keys to setting priorities.

There's the not-so-small matter of attitude: really wanting to accomplish a given task at a given time. How do you establish it?

## ESTABLISHING A "WANT-TO" THAT PAYS
## OFF IN SUSTAINED EFFORT

Priorities often depend on whether you are asking or giving. If you're demanding the action, your priority and time factors are twice as important as the other man's. If he is demanding action of you, you often give such a job half the priority that he does. The difference lies in who wants the action.

Establishing priorities can prevent chaos in your work routine. It can also help any assignment get the attention it deserves, and help establish for you a reputation for getting things done.

Claude Bolling didn't get to be division manager of the flight test area of an aircraft company by accident. One way that he earned it was through knowing how to establish a desire in his men to take an action that he felt necessary. For example, he was having trouble with his men breaching safety rules. His supervisors fussed and harped with no effect.

One day a mechanic was working in a wing section when someone started a small motor. The motor activated a drive shaft which grabbed the man's clothes and stripped them off his back—all of them! He was left wearing a pair of shoes and a smile, but was not hurt.

After the immediate excitement died down, Claude brought in a photographer and discreetly took pictures of the setting, the clothes and the man himself. He then set up meetings and showed all of his people what could happen when safety was ignored. He made them want something for themselves. Safety immediately took top priority—people stopped walking on wings without harnesses; they stopped activating motors without checking the surrounding area. That's why Claude's a good manager: establishing a want got his job and ideas attention.

A man's response to work is determined by the nature of the work, who referred it, and the timing. His attitude toward the task tells you of its importance.

Bill kept saying: "I haven't time for the work on Project X. All these little details keep popping up. I've only eight hours a day. I can't get my other work done. It doesn't have priority." He was being paid to do a job that included Project X. No matter which words he used, he only meant, "The priority is low." When priority gets too low, he had better turn it over to someone else, or stop and take stock. His manager must see that Bill isn't giving it priority and take action.

The priority given to certain tasks that are part of a man's job tell you about his attitude. If it is low priority, then it's something seen as interfering with his job. High priority is something else.

Maude Mueller was wrong—the saddest words of deed or pen are "I'm sorry, I've been too busy to do it." Don't fall into the easy trap of uttering these words or being caught by them. Establish a desire to do your work.

## HOW TO PLAN IN ORDER OF IMPORTANCE AND AVOID COSTLY DELAYS

Some people have just got it and others haven't. The action-getter is among those who have.

What has he got?

How does one person accomplish twice as much as another in the same time? An answer popped into my mind while watching my daughter Susan cook hot dogs.

She had brought in groceries and as she set the packages down, she turned on the stove. Then she turned on the hot water, got some hot dogs, put them in a pot, put them on the stove, and then put away the groceries. She's a home-grown efficiency expert.

An important thread of management in Susan's actions is that she had weighed the order of actions to avoid wasted time. Perhaps as managers, we should look at correct order of activities to get the most accomplished. You need to set first things first to provide correct lead time.

My secretary stated excitedly one day, "Oh, I can't wait to get our new supply cabinet."

"Have you ordered it yet?" I asked.

"No," she said, "Oh, I can't wait to *order* our new supply cabinet."

That's deciding what comes first.

As well as managers, a salesman must be result oriented and must set priorities in order of importance to conserve his time.

Bill Todd didn't. He began administering details of the sales and handling arrangements, but cut down the time spent in actual face-to-face selling. True, details have to be handled, but not to that degree. He lost confidence in his face-to-face encounters and took refuge in administrative work. Instead of confronting the problem, he let his sales drop off until he finally had to quit. The answer was only apparent after the fact. He rationalized that as long as he was doing something, he was working productively. However, the rest of his activity was wasted unless he was signing a contract and getting money in hand.

He would meet a friend on the street and spend an hour with him, maybe even have lunch with him. Time was lost because Bill didn't know how to get loose. Why not pass congenial conversation and move on? After all, Bill was heading to call on a customer at the time. It's easy to pass the time of day with people and not sell or move.

Every manager ought to spend some time selling door to door or doing some other personal contact selling. This experience gives a first-hand opportunity to see how much action pays off in how much money. A salesman very quickly discovers that if he doesn't make a certain number of calls and doesn't generate a certain amount of business, this company's income will decrease proportionately. It is easy, on the other hand, to work in a large business where a straight salary is paid and become accustomed to the salary coming in regardless of the amount of work expended or effectiveness produced in the job.

Guy Shealy, now vice president of a large company, spent years selling, budgeting his time, gauging results and learning self-discipline. He learned the value of his own time, how to set priorities, and in a period of eight years moved from salesman to vice president.

If every man in a big business could be required to ask himself what he had brought in for the company, or how his efforts have paid off each day, he might soon generate more action in favor of the company. He might end up making larger profits too.

Plan in order of importance so your time gets results.

## RELATING INTEGRITY TO DELIVERY WILL
## GET PROMPT RESULTS

Sam Shape called Jim William's office for a paper he had been promised. Jim's secretary said, "He's out of town."

"But he must have left it. He is one of the most dependable men around. If he says it will be delivered on such and such a date, it will be. Look around his desk and let me know."

She called back and said "It's not anywhere." This was unusual for a man with impeccable follow-through: who demands and gets action; who sets priorities.

In ten minutes a second call followed from Jim's secretary. "It's here. It just arrived air mail from New York."

"New York?"

"Yes, Mr. Williams was called out of town suddenly, and completed the paper on the plane." His batting average was still 1,000: he never fails to deliver the goods.

Finishing an action should be part of one's integrity. Jim Williams was selected from several hundred qualified men to become assistant to the president of the company. His uncompromising integrity was a part of the reason. If he promised action, he got it.

Show your men that delivery on time is a close relative to integrity. It can boost their production and your action-getting reputation.

## HOW TO BEG, BORROW, OR STEAL "AUTHORITY"
## TO GET PRIORITY

The man with authority in your area may not have the desire to help, may have other irons in the fire, or may be out to lunch. Perhaps it would take a whip to get priority for your project. Use somebody else's authority. This takes confidence and in some cases, nerve; but it works.

Joe Nichols, administrative supervisor, had charge of a project in manufacturing. He needed some carpentry done but found a bad backlog in the carpentry shop. Joe had a deadline to meet and needed a huge wooden sign by the following week. After he saw that he wouldn't make it, he went to Marion Trusten, the manager, and said, "The sign is a part of the upcoming property accounting program that Roy Settle is installing." Actually it was, but Roy didn't know the details. Roy was a big wheel who let someone else take care of the details. Marion said, "In that case, we'll try to get it for you." Joe got results by borrowing or stealing Roy's authority. He also got credit for having the project finished on time.

The executives in an aircraft plant wanted to reward good workmen with a flight in the company plane, but they were stymied by details, cost and selection criteria. Bill Tibbets, a group supervisor of management development, had tried for several years to get some of the executives interested in doing this. Now someone was needed to make the idea work. Bill drew up a plan. He assigned some of the already existing committees in the various departments as selection committees for the plane ride. He set up the first trip and even planned the date it would be made. Then he wrote up the plan, took it to two vice presidents. They bought it. If he hadn't just taken the authority to develop a plan, it would not have been done. The executives appreciated it, and Bill got to implement his pet project. His borrowed authority got his project approval and priority.

If you're right and *know* you're right, wade in and take over the authority needed to get the job done. It'll put you on the action-getting team.

## HOW TO GO TO ANY LEVEL NECESSARY
## TO BREAK LOGJAMS

A logjam is like just that. Many projects funnel into a department and cause a jam which affects workers, time and money. Somebody has got to grab a grappling hook and break the jam. If you have a project tied up in the mess, put on your lumberjack coat and get in there. You may have to bring someone else into the act to get it done. This is what happened when Joe Nichols used Roy Settle's name and authority. However, there are cases when you need the man himself.

George Currey is the manager in charge of the avionics on an aircraft under construction. He'd been concerned about a wiring problem for weeks, but all the people who should have been listening turned deaf ears. It would cost too much to put in a checking system, they said, besides, "We don't feel the situation is that bad." George stood it as long as he could and then went to a Quality Assurance Board Meeting for help. He broached the subject again and listened while the manufacturing engineer sloughed it off with "the situation isn't really that bad." George turned red in the face and said to the chairman, who was also the plant superintendent, "That's the dumbest thing I ever heard, and it's time you took a look." The chairman ordered a full report at the next meeting and discovered that there was indeed a need to take action. George got priority for his problem by having the nerve to bring in another level of authority. He got credit for the improvement and the chairman's praises for a job well done.

There comes a time to stand up and be counted—when you're right. Take your courage in hand, stand up and demand that the higher-up look closely at the logjam. He should discover that you've gone as far as you can without his help. That's what he is there for—to step in whenever you really need him. He'll appreciate your dedication to getting his project where it belongs.

## ESTABLISHING WHO'S GOING TO TELL
## HIM WHICH JOB COMES NEXT

*You* are of course! But what if he works for the other fellow, or—even worse—what if several of his bosses might be on the same project and the man doesn't know which to take orders from? Establish with him which assignments come first.

The worst example is a committee where many of you are doing many things. It must be clear which one gives orders to whom in representing the committee. Your project can become scrambled eggs if you don't make it clear who'll tell the man which job comes next.

The art department of a manufacturing company received a contract for a series of papers for the State Department of Education. These papers were intricate and involved input from six or seven areas of the plant. In the beginning, the supervisor was swamped with ideas, conflicting priorities, and frustrating changes. Jack Parker, the administrative supervisor for the area, had weathered such storms before. In order for the men to get the work done, someone had to set priorities. Jack merely asked that all input and priorities flow through Thealia's desk. She tied in all the details, decided which changes preceded which and managed to get this unruly job straight. Everyone knew that she determined which job came next. Jack again proved his ability to make order out of chaos.

When in doubt, establish who's going to determine the order of upcoming work. This can avoid trouble and get work out on time.

A large gathering of manufacturing engineers was planned. Jack Dabney was appointed manager. He put Ed Estrumse in charge of all dealings with the hotel. It made operations easy, since the hotel had to deal with only one man.

If any priority was needed to get action from the hotel, the members paged Ed. He told them which job came next. The result was a very smooth session. Jack received kudos from all over the country.

In any situation where several people have authority, the worst thing you can do is not establish priorities. The poor man that has an assignment could end up listening to one person and then another. Do him and the project a favor; tell him who to listen to.

## HOW YOUR SYMPATHY FOR HIS WORK LOAD WILL GET PRIORITY

When a man is swamped, he likes a little sympathy for his overwhelming work load. But if you are like I am your first thought is "So what, that's what he's paid for." That's the kind of thinking that will move your project to the very bottom of the stack.

Gregg Straighter supervises a group of clerks at the Georgian Art Company. Joe Deal owns an art store and orders supplies from them, but always gets complaints. Invariably, he is told "how busy the people are;" "the computer broke down;" "people are out sick;" "our own supplies haven't come in;" "there's a backlog of work" and so on. Joe learned that the best way to get results with Gregg and the others was by sympathizing with their situation.

He tried approaches like, "I know you are swamped;" "I'm sure the computer is backlogged;" "I know your supplies haven't come in." Then he'd ask if they could pull his order so he could pick it up. The answer usually was "O.K., we'll try it." Joe got his supplies when he needed them while similar shops waited in line for the spirit to move the clerk.

Humor your men a bit. Remember in the long run you are only after results and if a little bit of sympathy will do it, that is a small price.

## HOW HELP WITH SOME OF HIS PROBLEMS WILL HELP WITH YOUR PRIORITY

The next best thing to sympathy is help. Do a little something for your man—he'll love it. In fact, he'll feel obligated to reciprocate.

—Can you get some typing done for him?
—Drop off a package on the way back to the plant?
—Give a message to a man in the next department?
—Help him figure out a better delivery schedule?

Why not help him a little? It won't kill you.

The silk screen department was snowed under with urgent orders. Henry Arnell, manager had his hands full. Marketing needed the brochures in a hurry; Engineering needed charts; everybody needed something fast. Then along came Sargeant Foster wanting Air Force posters in a hurry. He got them first, because Foster helped Henry with a big problem—his tomatoes. They had a long talk right in the middle of Henry's busy schedule and Henry said, "Foster, my tomatoes are turning yellow and not bearing." Foster also grows tomatoes and long ago learned about nematodes. "Henry, get some nematode poison," he recommended. Henry was delighted. Foster had the poster by Wednesday. Foster knew enough to take time out and talk about Henry's interest and problems.

Do the same and trigger action. Help with his problem or work on his interest. You'll be surprised how fast your priority rises to the top of the list.

## HOW TO MAKE STRONG ASSIGNMENTS THAT OVERCOME "OUT OF SIGHT, OUT OF MIND"

As John Newman, President of Cartersville Bank says, "There are many ways to skin a cat, particularly when you're holding the knife and the skin." There are many ways to control an assignment:

L. B. Thompson, Manager of Fabrication Inspection, has crews of workers in four different buildings. He just can't look at each crew every day. One way that he keeps an eye on all projects is by having a short meeting every morning in which each supervisor reports just where he stands. If there are any areas in which he needs L.B.'s help, L.B. goes to those areas first. This keeps his men in direct communication. They know they're in the front of his mind even though out of sight most of the day.

As you know, it's seldom possible to make an assignment and forget it.

Dick Hamm does printing in his home, does good work, and will come over to pick up the copy. His service is reasonably priced. How can you beat that? The only drawback is that he sometimes drags along in delivery several days. Jim Tatum, who runs a small office equipment store, has learned how to handle him.

"Dick, if these aren't ready by June 2, I won't be able to use them and can't pay for them." When he hears that, Dick makes it on time. No one needs to be around to remind him. Jim doesn't have to make another move.

Joe Sheppard, a floor supervisor, assigned two men to reconstruct an aircraft center wing section that was broken in testing. He asked them to check with him when the bulkhead was removed and when the new one was ready to install. He controlled the assignment and got correct results faster.

Chuck West, Manager of Financial Counseling, assigned Johnny Robinson to reconcile outstanding loans. This meant several days work for Johnny in another part of the plant. Chuck knew that he himself would be out of the plant many times during the period. This meant that Johnny would be on his own. Knowing that Johnny fell behind at times, Chuck set up a schedule: "on Thursday all accounts should be listed and balanced; Friday take the report to Sue for typing." He then let Sue know they'd be coming her way. He even said, "Sue, call Johnny on Thursday and let Johnny know you'll be ready for the accounts Friday." It worked: the report was on time and Chuck passed it on to his manager, who was pleased with the reporting. Chuck could have been in trouble if Johnny hadn't come through. He reinforced the assignment to be sure to compensate for the "out of sight, out of mind" factor.

In getting action, consider what *could go wrong*—then establish some control to catch and correct it. If you're away, the effort will pay.

## TAKING HIS TEMPERATURE TO SEE WHERE YOUR JOB STANDS ON HIS LIST

Find out whether your project is hot or cold. It could just lie there like unleavened bread. Look for symptoms that will tell you if your project is being ignored.

Marie Bledsoe is head of the teletype room and has to manage a large number of girls as well as control the ordering of supplies and negotiate equipment repairs. When one of the girls said that a machine was not functioning, Marie grabbed the phone and called the repairman. "We'll be over," the man said. Marie had heard that before, so she persisted: "What time?" "Well, we have two other repairs before yours." "What time will that be?" she asked. "Probably this afternoon," the man replied. Marie kept on, "I must know for sure whether to keep the girl the rest of the afternoon." "Better plan on tomorrow morning," he said. "Well, thanks anyway," Marie said. In this way she avoided the cost of another worker for the day. Marie learned that a little temperature taking saves time later.

A few well-placed and timely questions like those Marie used can avoid trouble later. Use such a line of questioning to take temperatures. If someone's cool, then take steps to build a fire under his desire for priority. It'll keep you out of the cold.

## BUILDING A FIRE UNDER SOMEONE ELSE'S WORKER KEEPS YOUR JOB HOT

Gerry Ramer is the manager of the Modifications Department and has people with line authority to other organizations operating in his area. For example, he manages people from Quality Assurance, Maintenance and Engineering in a functional sense, but has no line authority over them. Therefore Gerry is constantly looking for ways to inspire them. Here are some of the ways in which he is successful:

—When he has a planning meeting, he invites them as if they were his own men.

—He sends them copies of all memos that concern their mutual operations.

—He has their office space in his area.

—He asks their advice before making many moves.

These men in turn support him and keep priority for modifications. Gerry, in turn, is recognized as a good manager.

George Kelly does the same in working on cargo ramps and floors. He is the swing shift manager and has to coordinate his work with several other organizations, notably mockup, blueprints cribs, and production control. He has tremendous pride in his people and really lets this be known across lines. He is always telling people, "Our shift is the best because we work as a team." It's contagious. Recently when the manager in Mockup had a job going for another section, George called him and said, "Mike, if we don't get this organized first, it could delay the assembly line." Mike told his people to switch over to George's job and move it out. They did, and George met his schedule. He personally went over to thank Mike and his staff. This kind of recognition has helped him to get assistance any time he needs it. He's an action-getter when it comes to priority.

Whether the workers are in functionally related jobs, as in George's and Gerry's cases, or whether they are providing a service from a completely separate organization as in Marie's situation, one fact is foremost: you're the one that'll look bad if they let you down. Crying about it later won't make up for missed action. Gear up to get action while there is still time, even if it means building a fire under someone else's workers.

## HOW TO GET A SMALL COMMITMENT, THEN GO FOR A BIG ONE AND PRODUCE PRIORITY

The men in purchasing are supposed to handle all buying for the company. They sometimes relinquish some purchasing authority to the Office Equipment Department or Supplies Department, but they do the greatest part of the buying, such as contracting and subcontracting. Their main concern is to get the things necessary to keep production going. Anything else takes second priority.

Jim Tindall, group supervisor in Field Service knew this and needed their help. He was in the process of selling refurbishing kits to the government. These kits needed small wooden boxes that would have to be bought outside. Jim called Jack Place and said, "I need your advice in getting some boxes." Jack said, "O.K., come on over Tuesday at 10:00." Jim got Jack to discuss possible sources and prices, and even call one of the subcontractors to get his quote. Jack finally said, "I'll get Dale to help you follow this through and get what you need."

If Jim had called and proposed buying the boxes, Jack would have been reluctant to help. He probably would have told him as they had many others that "We are too busy buying production goods to fool with that." He had other things to do. Jim got action by asking for just a little at the time. He also made the man feel important. In the process he got priority for his seemingly insignificant project.

Don't ask for the big commitment. Ask for the small, seemingly unimportant one. Once you get the man to help or think in terms of what you want, get commitment for all your needs.

The Technical Printing Department had a contract and a deadline. There were really too few people to get instruction books printed in time for a vocational school contract. It was necessary to get help wherever it was available. Frank Schuman a group supervisor was smart. He needed Rick Tewell's help to relieve several people, but Rick was already busy and disclaimed any part in the project. Frank went to him and asked him to merely check the grammar in the chapters that had been completed. Before long, Frank had Rick not only checking grammar but rewriting. He became a valuable member of the team. This happened because Frank got him involved in a small commitment. It was then easy for Rick to take a bigger step. Rick felt he was needed and really plunged into the effort, taking charge of the editing of the whole project. The result was excellent. Frank got the project out on time and the directors of the vocational school implemented the instruction books immediately. The local director of the County Area Vocational School called Frank's boss to congratulate him on the quality of the product and the efficient way that Frank had handled the contract. Getting results from recalcitrant members such as Rick was a large part of his success. Head for the small commitment first, and then it won't be as hard to reach for larger ones.

## HOW TO APPEAL TO HIS SENSE OF
## FAIR PLAY AND GOOD WORKMANSHIP

When I needed wire fencing to be installed around the back of a store I went to a department store. They gave me a quote and a promise that they would come out and measure the place. Two weeks later they hadn't come, so I called again. This time they came and measured, but said the price had gone up. They also said it would take six weeks to get the job done. This was rather aggravating. I reminded them that if they'd come when they were supposed to I would have had the old price and two weeks' start, and that was what I expected. The representative saw the point and agreed. I got a better deal and quicker delivery. Appeal to the sense of fair play if necessary.

There's also the question of good workmanship. If it's not up to par, one way to get priority for a rework is to appeal to pride. Claude Frank delivered the printed material to Bill Tibbets on time but with smears. He told Bill that there was no time to do it over. Bill wouldn't have any part of that. He said, "Claude, you wouldn't want the managers to assume that this is one of your standards." Claude admitted, "No, now that you put it like that, I wouldn't." "Well, let's redo it then," stated Bill. Claude agreed.

If a man has any sense of pride in his workmanship, appeal to it. It can help you get your work redone and up to standards. Your people need to be able to make that same appeal. Don't let them settle for less than the best: then if a rework comes along, it will take priority. Suppose Claude had said, "I'll redo it, but we are terribly busy now, so it'll have to wait." Keep in mind that he made the mistake, so the redo should take precedent over other work. Let him know it graciously but in no uncertain terms. You're after a certain quality; hang in there until you get it. Your work deserves top priority.

## KNOWING WHEN TO TAKE A PROJECT
## OFF OF THE FRONT BURNER

There comes a time to stop pushing, particularly if your project has decreased in importance. Take it off the front burner and give someone else a break. There will be another time, and you'll want to have him ready to help you. He'll appreciate the breather.

Herb Spring has the respect of all of the service organizations in the company. When he does need something done, they usually pitch in and give him priority. That didn't just happen: he had to earn their respect. For example, Herb, who manages an aircraft supply program in the product support organization, heard that a special Air Force project was being cancelled. One of the top marketing people had passed this along to him as reliable information, yet it could be several days until he got official notice. In the meantime repair bulletins were being produced at a breakneck pace for this project. Herb's first thought was of Art DeLong and his staff. He called Art and said, "I can't tell you for sure, but I think the project is being cancelled. Put the bulletins on the back burner until we get word." The notice came in a couple of days and additional work was not wasted. Art thanked Herb for letting him know promptly.

This is how Herb continues to get action and manage successfully.

Push when need be but let up the moment that there is no need and you'll win friends and influence service organizations.

## CREATING CONVENIENCE AS A STATE OF MIND

When a person says it isn't convenient to do something, he may just not want to do it. The moment he does, it is convenient.

Being out of town isn't an excuse for nonperformance; neither is being too busy. Having your time pre-empted by the boss, or being in the hospital are not excuses—they're reasons. However, there are few acceptable reasons for lack of performance or notification. It is easy for a man to perform or give you notice if he really wants to.

Three men walked into the classroom at two- or three-minute intervals, five and ten minutes late. The guest lecturer stopped, went over, introduced himself, and said, "Glad you could be with us." He did this in his best tones, no hint of sarcasm; and yet they'll think twice before coming in late again. They just didn't leave home in time. Late once—accident; twice—habit; three times—a state of mind. Convenience is the same.

The same applies to absences—state of mind. The nice thing about saying "I couldn't be there, I was sick," is that no one is supposed to question it because if you say you were sick, you *were* sick. Here's the dividend: you are also supposed to get sympathy. Doesn't everyone always sympathize with the sick?

Next time some deadline must be met, be sick and don't show up. No one can question it and you'll get sympathy. Of course it's even harder to deal with that distasteful element the next time around because you lost a little psychological ground.

Any time we hear someone say "It isn't convenient" to go to the Kiwanis meeting or to church or whatever, he's really saying "I don't want to."

Bill Tibbets, the management development supervisor discovered he could get results by making something convenient—by making the person want to do it. He kept trying to get a model airplane from the marketing support department and every time he was told that it couldn't be done then because they were too busy. After all, Project Design had in a request for six models and Public Relations needed four. This happened twice before Bill caught on.

He called Jim Lansfort, the Marketing Support representative, and said, "Hey Jim, I am going to have a meeting with the members of Structures and Aeronautics. They should have a model of their plane to keep in their meeting room. Can you come over for about five minutes and discuss our current marketing efforts and present them with a model?" Jim said, "I'd love to. What time is it?"

It's strange how supply becomes more plentiful, time becomes abundant and things are easier to do when a man wants to do it. Go to work on his want-to and make your project convenient. Convenience is often the same as priority.

Here's a quick recap of some of the efforts that you can make in order to speed up your project:

a. Plan in order of importance.
b. Show the relationship between integrity and delivery.
c. Beg, borrow or steal authority.

d. Give the man you're trying to get action from your help and sympathy.
e. Take his temperature to determine where your job rates, and then build a fire under him if necessary. If your project cools down, take it off the front burner.

# 7

## INSTILLING RESPONSIBILITY AND GETTING INVOLVEMENT FOR REAL RESULTS

The successful completion of any job demands commitment. You can get this from your people but it isn't easy. It's worth your extra effort, however, since their responsibility and involvement will get you real results.

Consider the way two different girls handle phone calls. Both reflect the philosophy of their managers. One works for a man who spends little time instilling a responsibility for results. The other works for a manager that holds his people responsible for satisfying his customers. Here's the first one:

"This is Sam Tillman. May I speak with John Doakes?"

"He's not here." (Period, and that's that) It's aggravating to terminate a call on such a note with no assistance, politeness or information. Sam continued.

"Is he dead?"

"No," she replied, with all seriousness, "He's not in the office."

"Did you fire him?" By this time the little lady realized that there was something she was not doing for the caller so she said:

"No, he's at a meeting. Can I take a message?" Ahhh, now she's decided to help.

What do you think of her manager? Is he the action-getting type? Would you rate him as successful? This certainly isn't the message you want radiating from your office.

All isn't lost, though; listen to this one:

A long distance call came for Frank Schoffield, R.C.A., Camden, New Jersey. A young lady answered:

> "I'm sorry, he isn't in. May I take a message?"
> "Yes, have him call me when he comes in," and the caller left his name and number.

> A few minutes later, the phone rang and another lady said, "I'm Mr. Schoffield's secretary. I was out when you called and another person took the message. Mr. Schoffield won't be back for several days and I felt I should let you know in case you had an immediate need and someone else could help. Mr. Schoffield doesn't like his calls to wait."
> You can't resist telling the young lady, "Thanks for being so considerate."

That's a satisfying feeling, to be treated with that much consideration and on long distance at that!

You may say, "Those girls were born that way." Not at all: they work in completely different environments with different standards.

The first girl, Jo, works in an organization with low standards. The manager lets people operate as they please; he's never mentioned phone courtesy or any other kind. He's never discussed customer satisfaction. In fact, his policy is noninterference. If Jo had come to the job with high standards, it would have been helpful, but unfortunately, she didn't—she couldn't care less. Pity her poor customers.

The second girl, Kate, works for a demanding manager who constantly discusses the needs and desires of the people who deal with his organization. He holds weekly meetings to talk about the organization's output, and helps each of his people to feel a part of the organization personally and a responsibolity for its total output and direction. He makes his people believe they *are* the company; he instills responsibility.

You can instill responsibility and get involvement for real results by using these tested guidelines:

1. Develop job identification.
2. Sell legitimate interruptions as part of the job.
3. Show an employee how to consider customers' feelings.
4. Show him how to meet the other person more than half way.
5. Swap jobs for better understanding.
6. Show him how his work fulfills company objectives.
7. Use him to solve a problem.
8. Let him sell you on his job.
9. Appeal to his pride.
10. Get him to feel it is his company.
11. Talk about his past successes.

Examine more closely how these and other guidelines can work for you in creating involvement and instilling responsibility.

## HOW TO DEVELOP JOB IDENTIFICATION
## SO A MAN WILL ACCEPT RESPONSIBILITY

Identification leads to responsibility: this is your base for action. Start by working on job identification. One way to develop job identification is by constantly reminding your people that they are responsible for the final results.

John Smith's philosophy is as straightforward as his name. He's manager of a fabrication plant where aircraft parts are assembled and installed. One thing he constantly impresses on his supervisors is their responsibility for parts being on the line at the right time. He knows that it is easy for men to get involved in their particular assignments and say, "Well, that is in his area, let him look after it," or "leave the rest to Joe."

John Smith works on total job responsibility. It is best seen when a late job comes in and must move fast to prevent a line shortage. He follows this pattern:

- He gets commitment from each supervisor as to when he will complete his part of the job.
- Each supervisor learns when the others must have the part.
- The supervisors then meet with their people so that all involved get the facts fast from their own bosses.
- They are all held mutually responsible for getting the work done.

- Progress is posted on the bulletin board.
- Final schedule and records of their time spent are shown and the picture of accomplishment for the whole department is posted.

Each man is identified with the job and they get real results. You can use the same identification to get responsible action. In the fabrication organization, James Moore manages the metal bonding section. He believes in creating responsibility by giving a man plenty of information so that he can thoroughly identify with the job at hand. He *tells* his men:

- The hours they will be allowed to use.
- Complete instructions.
- Date due out.
- Dollars and cents cost of any parts damaged.
- Causes of any errors that must be corrected.
- Examples of any good work in the area that deserves recognition.
- The reasons for special procedures.

As a result, his men know what they are doing and why, and are really identified with their work. You will get results by helping your employees understand all aspects of their jobs so that they become committed to it.

## A SUCCESSFUL TECHNIQUE FOR GETTING A MAN TO ACCEPT RESPONSIBILITY

Joe Bostwick, in the same fabrication department, is an older manager who controls the electrical wiring that goes into the parts. He has learned a clever and very specific way to get job identification. *He lets all of his people who have shown good workmanship stamp their own work.* This means that a man's signature says his job is done right, and that he accepts full responsibility for his own work. The employees are thrilled at the chance to sign their own jobs. That is real job identification!

Consider possible ways that your men can inspect their own work or verify it with their signatures. This causes a personal link between the man and his product or service.

Responsibility works with children as well as adults. Two couples got together to play bridge. There was no one to babysit, so one couple brought their children with them. Their two, together with the host's two children, nearly tore the house down. It was impossible to play any bridge. Several attempts by parents failed to quiet them or get any semblance of order. Finally, Jim Lunsford, a manager in a chemical company, went out of the room for a few minutes. From the moment he came back there was absolute quiet. Finally, one of the wives asked, "How did you do it?"

"Simple," replied Jim, "I took each one out of the room separately and told him, "I'm looking to you personally to keep the rest of that group under control—that's going to be your job." Each one felt responsible for the others.

Your people will act the same if they feel well enough identified with results to make a plan work.

The key in these examples is spelling out responsibility and enforcing it, both for total job and for each piece of work that comes through. By doing this you get job identification and responsible action.

## HOW YOU CAN SELL LEGITIMATE INTERRUPTIONS AS A PART OF THE JOB AND GET A BETTER WORK PERSPECTIVE

Most supervisors will agree that anybody can handle a job if he isn't bothered by customers and other people. However, those jobs are few and far between. Most of the people working for you have to deal with people, and consequently are faced with interruption of any planned work. This is a way of life: it is an important part of their job. The involved worker takes a legitimate interruption as a momentary detour from his planned work and sees the need to handle it correctly. Joe Pearce, manager of a parts supply house, raised the question, "How many times have supervisors said and heard, 'I could get much more accomplished if I could cut out the interruptions.' Joe adds that all of his supervisors must understand that today's management is by exception, and that legitimate interruptions are exceptions. The handling of the exceptions shows the real ability of the action-oriented manager. Illegitimate interruptions—people who stop by to shoot the breeze or otherwise take time—need to be weeded out. These people need to be courteously but firmly sent on their way. Normal interruptions could take the form of equipment breakdowns, production setbacks, quality deficiencies, safety hazards cropping up, or complaining customers. Here's where his supervisors develop their mettle. You can condition your men to deal with interruptions.

Of course, some people consider any customer activity as interfering with their jobs:

> When he needed a new window screen, Jim McDade called several shops. The X store told him it had one in size 32 by 54 inches. He would have preferred, if possible, one that was a half inch wider. He called another branch of X store and the man said he didn't have the right size nor did he believe the other branch had a 32 by 54 inch screen: it was not a standard size, he said.
>
> Jim called a third X branch store and got the same response. He called back to the first store and asked the man again about that size.
>
> "Yes, that's right," he said.
>
> "Would you mind measuring one before I make the eight-mile round trip to get it?"
>
> "I'm sorry," the man said. "I can't. They're *down there* and I'm *up here.*"
>
> "Well, is there someone *down there* who could check it?" Jim asked.
>
> "Yes," he said, *"But they're all busy."*
>
> "Well, I hope they are," Jim replied. "If they're playing checkers you should fire them. I hate to drive eight miles unless you are positive."
>
> "O.K.," the man said, finally, "Wait a minute." He put his hand over the phone and yelled to the other manager. In a minute he said in an apologetic tone, "I'm sorry, you're right. They're not 32 by 54."
>
> "Thanks, buddy."

Imagine telling Jim his people were busy! Does that mean Jim's interfering with their work? As a customer, he is their work. The manager is setting a bad example for his people which will permeate the organization. The interruptions should be part of their work if their perspective is correct.

Your actions could set the same example. Be sure it's positive when dealing with others.

## HOW TO SET A POSITIVE EXAMPLE
## IN HANDLING INTERRUPTIONS

Jim Williamson sets a different kind of pattern for his people. As manager of a large sales force in a manufacturing company, he's one of the busiest men I've ever seen. Yet just call on the man and watch his tempo and approach. He takes you in as though he has nothing else whatsoever to do, and gives you his undivided attention and help. He closes the door and asks his secretary to hold the calls. Of course, he then puts a reasonable limit on his time, but while you're there he doesn't give you any inkling of interference with his routine. His people have learned this from him and consequently work harmoniously with people. He's influenced their attitudes.

The attitudes of your people can make the difference between an interruption and what they were paid to handle in the first place. Help them make it their job and get the right kind of action.

## HOW CUSTOMER EMPATHY EXTENDS
## RESPONSIBLE ACTION

The writer of a popular song said "Walk a mile in my shoes." If you can get your people to honestly look at things from the other person's perspective they'll come a lot closer to fulfilling their responsibility to get action.

John Vinson manages a real estate company. His salesmen take their cue from him. Recently a man who rented a store from him was quite demanding in what he wanted included. John didn't give away everything, but he considered the other man's feelings very closely: the man was putting his life savings into the place and he probably would make a good go of it. He used customer empathy. When a small partition was needed, John agreed, saying it would be twice as difficult and expensive for the renter to put it in. His men could do it while finishing the interior of the building. He also agreed to several other items that would have cost the renter time and money.

The concessions cost John comparatively little, and yet convinced the renter that John was genuinely interested in his success. As a result he has persuaded a friend to rent in the shopping center, without realizing that he was doing John a favor. In the long run, John gets back in good will and advertising every cent he spends considering the customer's feelings. His men have learned to put themselves in the customer's shoes.

Pass on to your people this same consideration. Discuss with them every situation in which they did well or in which they could have been more helpful. Help them to honestly see the other person's side of a situation.

## TRAINING YOUR PEOPLE TO MEET CUSTOMER'S NEEDS WITH ONE SIMPLE QUESTION

Sally Corbet, the assistant manager of a loan company, can find innumerable ways to help people. She always thinks in terms of the customer's needs and feelings, arranges suitable terms, postpones payments if necessary, makes out new terms, substitutes collateral and does limitless jobs to meet the customer's demands. I've never heard her say, "There's no way to work that out!" She is a positive action-getter and works to satisfy the customer's wants. She can really see his side and consider what's in it for him.

Customer identification is as important as job identification. Your people can be trained to think in terms of the customer's feelings. If you are not selling, there must still be some interaction between your employees and others—at least among themselves. They will be more effective in getting responsible action if you show them how to consider the feelings of others.

One effective way to get your workers trained to talk and think in terms of the customer's feelings is the phrase: "What is in it for the customer?" Each time the employee talks about a product or service, get him to answer this question, until it becomes a habit.

For example, consider the statement: "It is made of highly polished brass." What is in that for the customer? "He'll have equipment that looks good on his fireplace." *Or:* "This paint is acrylic." What's in it for the customer? "He can mix it and clean it up with water, avoiding the mess of turpentine and oil."

"This form must be filled out and returned with the statement." What is in it for the other fellow? "You'll be sure that you get credit for all of the work done." Try it on your people; it'll work wonders.

## REMOVING TIGHT MENTAL BOUNDARIES
## AND ENLARGING A MAN'S CONCEPT

As a successful manager you can get action by enlarging the concepts of your employees. This means extending the boundaries of what they can do, motivating them by letting them see a total picture, and most importantly, putting themselves in that picture. Work on their attitudes in order to get top performance.

Mark Brown had to get his organization through a critical stress survey test by the time the accounting period and the contract for the test program ended.

When he started to work to make this particular test successful, he took several positive steps:

1. He got all of his people together, including his supervisors.
2. He discussed all the requirements for the critical test.
3. He carefully broke the requirements down into specifics such as open work, job setup, hydraulic jacks and plumbing, lead-in systems, and others.
4. He carefully showed each section its responsibility.

The supervisors were dumbfounded by the hours that would be needed to run the tests, but they started. Copying Mark's leadership, they sat down each day for a few minutes to see if there were any problems that needed solving or any ideas for ways to minimize time. By starting early and working late, they successfully reached their deadline.

Mark took the extra time to condition his men mentally. He also expanded their conceptions of what they could do. The result was success. Your success as a manager depends to a great extent on the concepts of your people. Test your workers to see the extent of their thinking. You can step in at any time and help them see a larger picture or remove obstacles.

A common infectious disease in any large company is "compartmentitis." It's got many carriers and results in tight mental boundaries. The manager says, "Let's do our job and let the chips fall where they may. Let the guys down the line worry about themselves." In the long run this disease can really increase expenses.

You can avoid it if you help your people see their own work clearly, while breaking down tight mental boundaries of what they can and can't do.

The subassemblies were hard to work in Area A, so shims were put on each part to make it fit. Chris Goodyear, manager in the major subassembly department of the production company, jumped down off the work platform one day and said, "enough!" He was tired of his men in Area A taking the blame for all of the things that were going wrong. It seemed they didn't know how to work the parts and the inspectors were complaining about the shims. Chris was convinced the problem was coming to them from another area and was not content to just let them solve it themselves, and so he made his move:

He went to the next department and watched the work.

He stood up on the highest work deck and squeezed stringers together.

He watched several men riveting.

Sure enough, the assemblies were buckling because the men were riveting stringer B ahead of stringer A. It was easier for them to get to the stringers in that order.

Chris called the other department manager aside and showed him what was wrong. The other manager agreed quickly to change it and reverse the riveting order. This removed the slight buckle and eliminated the need for shims in Chris' department.

Chris could have kept his people working the assemblies and merely shifted blame to the other department. Instead, he went past the boundaries and corrected the causes. His example will stick in the minds of his workers and influence them to do likewise.

You can instill responsibility by setting this sort of example and assuring that your employees have the right concept rather than "compartmentitis."

## SHOWING HIM HOW TO MEET THE OTHER PERSON MORE THAN HALF WAY

Who takes the initiative? Who gets the action? If your employee is serving someone else, he does. If he intends to get action he'd better take the initiative. You want him to meet the other person more than half way. Sally Corbet does this. So does John Vinson.

J. C. Hernandez owns and manages a wholesale supply house for arts and crafts. He knows how many stores have been set up. He knows turnover averages per year, percentage of sales made each month, mark-up, expenses and the goods that sell best.

He responds readily if someone calls on him for help, really meeting the man more than half way. J. C. identifies with the man starting a business and anticipates his needs and requirements. Will a few lead items at discount help the business get a good start? Will classes in handicrafts draw customers? It's almost as if he were starting his own business.

In turn, his customer buys with a high level of confidence, and people all over recommend J. C. His employees, in his absence, are completely competent. They might not be quite as knowledgeable as J. C., but they can go more than half way in helping the customer. They've long since caught his spirit.

You will always have satisfied customers if your people get the same spirit from you. Show them the necessity of going all out for the other fellow.

## INCREASING A PERSON'S UNDERSTANDING AND RESPONSIBILITY BY SWAPPING JOBS

You now have a fine training technique at your disposal which can instill responsibility by increasing your employees' understanding. Swap jobs with him. It can cost you a little money in the short run, because he's going to need time to learn and might make some mistakes. This is a small price to pay, however, for teaching him to be versatile. You will also be building his responsibility.

What does swapping jobs mean? Joe in the purchasing section supervises a group of girls checking in orders all day long. They process paper work and coordinate with the inventory system in the warehouse. Next door Jake and his group are placing orders. They deal with vendors, push late orders and do liaison work with the outside. Jake and Joe know only one side of the operation: If they are going to grow they need a more complete picture. Have them swap jobs. This will not only increase their understanding and responsibility, but will give them practice in supervising an entirely different group of people.

Russ Granger swears by this process. He manages the extrusion department of a production company, and has many cost centers within the department. It is almost essential that his supervisors be flexible. By rotating them to other jobs, they learn associated operations and crews, bring their own knowledge to new assignments, and visualize the department's total operation. He rotates them every four months until all have worked in all areas. He does the same with his hourly employees to improve their skills. An average of ten per month are upgraded either in his department or in another. Sometimes he loses good people, but the company gains.

Russ also gets his men to serve on various committees such as Corrective Action, so they can grow. In the process they learn how to get things done.

This process can create a better pool of brain power for you. One side of the house understands what the other side is all about. One large company has a contingent of engineers who constantly battle with production. What one designs and the other produces often seem at odds. Engineering sometimes designs something impossible to produce or inconsistent with schedules and facilities.

Vern Bennett, the production manager, went to the company president with a solution: job swapping. The president agreed. Vern put a top structural engineer, a top materials engineer, a manufacturing engineer and others in critical decision-making spots and gave them a chance to learn production. The difference in engineering recommendations and practicality was then apparent to them. He accomplished unity and understanding, promoting not only their growth, but the company's.

Pay the short-run price by letting a man try several jobs. You will get better overall involvement from your men if they thoroughly understand all parts of the whole.

Another engineer in a manufacturing company, Bob Roth, was moved to marketing. Everyone thought the company president, Dick Parker, was pushing it a little since Bob had no sales background or inclination. However, Dick knew better. Bob was put in Application Engineering, which was a half-breed department composed of engineers selling technical designs. This started him on the marketing road. He was then put in Military Sales, which allowed him to coordinate military requirements with marketing and engineering. In two years he moved into a manager's spot and five years later was promoted to vice president. He probably could never have mastered it without the thorough background experience that Dick gave him. Dick believes in swapping jobs for future benefit.

You can look down the line to plan several years ahead, and start moving your men now so they'll be ready. As we stated earlier, you may pay in the short run, but you and the company win in the long run

## HOW YOU CAN AVOID LOSING A GOOD MAN

Elliott Evans started a complete program within his metals fabrication company. Several young energetic members left the company because they were skeptical about growth and their own current status. Elliott discovered several things wrong in his organization. His men were bogged down in staff jobs: they were out of the mainstream of line management which needed them desperately. If they moved, it was never beyond department lines; any rotation was limited. Elliott decided to change all of that.

- He set up a committee of his managers.
- They selected 10 or 12 of the up-and-coming men.
- They planned a promotion system to cover several years.
- They set up a system of accountability that would make the moves happen regardless of current business or momentary trends.

In this way, Elliott's men received better training. One became a manager; several became supervisors; but most important, none left the company since it has become more progressive. If your men attain success, you'll attain success. Each time you help them advance, you enhance your own reputation as a manager who gets responsible action.

Bob Fowler took a circuitous route to becoming manager of property accounting in his company, and again, it was because of the vision of his manager. He completed years of schooling and co-op work. His education was tied to practice. After graduation he was given a staff job in production, but Ike Jenkins, Industrial Relations manager, watched him to be sure he didn't stagnate. Bob stayed in production several years to learn the scope of line management, but then Ike moved him to Industrial Engineering, where he learned the mechanics of setting up production. He then went on to a job in Finance to learn accounting, and finally became manager of Property Accounting. Ike has vision and allowed for Bob's growth. Needless to say Bob's feeling of responsibility is unequalled.

Whether you want to groom a man for future moves or are interested in his full involvement with responsibility right now, move him around to enlarge his understanding.

## ENHANCING HIS ROLE BY SHOWING HOW HIS WORK FULFILLS COMPANY OBJECTIVES

The old story about turning a bolt on the assembly line can really exist in industry, causing a man to deny any connection with the final product. It's hard to feel proud of the product when you turn a bolt all day long. Many jobs have about the same amount of reward or excitement. You've got to liven it up and help a man see a direct relation to the final product or company goals if he is to be motivated.

Jack Roquemore faced this problem with inspectors in a manufacturing company. Jack had been in the business for more than twenty years and knew the mental requirements. He needed a way to improve his men's identification with the product. His inspectors looked at an item, moved it along to mate with another which someone else inspected. The man stayed at his post, watched items become part of something else and move on. He couldn't identify with what happened. Jack decided to change that. He assigned the inspector to a part and the product as it moved along the line so he retained inspection responsibility, no matter who worked on it. He even hung the man's name on it. Jack saw pride increase tremendously, his man identified with company output and worked fiercely to protect his product from poor workmanship. The company product became his product. He worked to meet company objectives. Show your men how their work fits into the objectives of your company so they will stretch their thinking.

## IDENTIFICATION WITH TOTAL COMPANY OBJECTIVES

Charles Storch's personnel department moves masses of people and paper in a process that often gets long and drawn out.

- Prospective employees are interviewed.
- Paper work is placed in the files.
- Information is checked and recorded.
- Managers in appropriate areas are contacted and informed.
- Decisions are made and recorded.
- Applicants are notified of those decisions and those coming to work are given further instructions.

Procedures can tie up anyone. Charlie ran an informal survey and discovered that once a man started a piece of paper in the system, he lost interest in it. It became someone else's responsibility and if it bogged down, no one cared.

Charlie decided to change this. He started with Sue Dalton who contacts managers and helps with hiring decisions. She was the midway point in the process. He asked Sue to retain responsibility until the applicant is notified of disposition of the application—even if it travels through someone else's area. He heard such remarks as "We're running late because Mary Ann's desk takes two days to process the work" (Previously no one cared how long Mary Ann took) or, "There's a bottleneck in the notification group." (Then they began to iron out bottlenecks.) The result was an improvement in notification of potential new employees from ten days to four. And the orientation of new employees was set up on a timely basis. The difference came when individuals identified with company results rather than limited action. Charlie got his people "result oriented." That's what you're after: do the same by tying any action to final results. Show your man how his part in a process relates to company objectives.

This can be done on a big scale. A manufacturing company had a branch that made small parts and seemed to be a completely separate entity.

Joe Waters, manager in the parent plant decided that much better workmanship would be forthcoming if better ties were established between work in the branch and the parent company's objectives.

Another branch, also made small parts and seemed to live in their own world. The supervisors had never been to the main plant nor inspected the final product. Joe put his tie-in plan in action here. The branch supervisors were brought in for the weekend. They were taken to every corner of the large plant. Key people talked to them and became real to them. They saw the finished product and how their products fitted into it.

The results were improved coordination at the branch plant and meeting of schedules. The supervisors felt they were on one big schedule that all must meet. Joe has them motivated to work with the main plant and total company objectives.

Be sure that you take whatever time is necessary to show your men how their work fits. It's easy for the company to become a "they," disassociated from the working individual. Keep your men tied to the important objectives and get the right kind of action.

## USING HIM TO SOLVE A PROBLEM FOR REAL IMPROVEMENT

A man feels at his strongest when he can help someone do something. Did you ever think that when you let someone do something for you he usually welcomes the chance to help and there's a little stronger bond between you? Let him help solve some problems and he really becomes a company man.

In a manufacturing research organization many ways had been considered to stop using up white gloves. Manager Mack Stein called on two very competent men to help—one in his organization and one in purchasing. They devised a way of washing the gloves that enables them to be reused: it cleans all types, even expensive leather ones, puts them in order and packages them so that they're good as new. This saves almost half of the money previously spent on gloves, and the two men feel like masters for having helped with the solution. Get your men at all levels into problem solving—it's good for their morale, and nobody knows the answer better than men on the line.

George Alexander owns a small tooling company which manufactures jigs and fixtures used in building large products. These fixtures get misused and abused, banged up and torn apart. George looked for some way to keep them in operation with minimum repairs. He asked several of his first-line workers to solve this problem. They analyzed the quality problems from every angle and found improvements. One man discovered a better way to attach some of the movable parts so they could not be removed. Another suggested consolidation of parts in one area to prevent extra work. Not only did George get help in providing a more usable product, but his men also became more involved than ever in turning out top quality.

Look for any opportunity to turn a problem over to your men and let them solve it: you'll increase job identification and responsibility.

## LET HIM SELL YOU ON THE VALUE OF HIS WORK AND IT'LL TAKE ON GREATER MEANING

Things were rough in a certain manufacturing company: business was slack and morale was bad. Bob Osborne, who managed the engineering section of the company, was particularly concerned when he saw his men leave with bad feelings about the company. Highly motivated engineers lost heart. Bob developed a plan to help them over the rough time. He got them together, ostensibly to give them information, but really to improve their image of themselves until business improved and things got back to normal.

While he had them together, he asked each one to tell the group a little about his background and why the company needed his particular services. They really sold themselves. You could see morale rising. You heard such things as, "I'm the best design engineer in the business and can keep the product safe," and "I've had 25 years of structure engineering and can iron out problems before they happen."

This kind of action and thinking helped Bob to retain his best men through lean times. Nothing helps a man like having a chance to brag. Your men will certainly pick up their dedication whenever you give them a chance to tell you how good they are—they'd prove it or bust.

## HOW TO USE HIS KNOWLEDGE TO SELL YOUR IDEA

Al Evans manages several laboratories. He called one of his men before a senior planning council to discuss the need for money to support a machine in their lab. This man waxed eloquent when he started selling the value of his work. The committee caught his enthusiasm and voted the money, after Al had not been able to convince them. He was not as closely involved with the project since it was not his own personal work, but he was smart enough to let his man sell the value of his work.

Your people will respond to such questions as:

- How do you plan to . . . ?
- How will you do the . . . ?
- Where does the . . . go?
- Why is this essential?

Stand back and watch them go.

Bob Harrison, training manager in the Value Engineering Company has a unique way of determining how well a man understands a project or how much he is sold on it. He literally tricks the man into selling him on it. On the first approach the answer is liable to be "it won't work, I don't like it." This leaves the door open for the man to try again. Bob may resist the second time, but if his man persists, he knows that the man believes in it himself. A man loves to hear you tell him how good he is, but second to that he loves to tell you how good he is. Give him this chance and increase the meaning of his work.

## HOW TO APPEAL TO HIS PRIDE AND RAISE HIS LEVEL OF WORKMANSHIP

There's not a worker around that doesn't have pride. You can locate it and appeal to it. Perhaps the best way is through identification, as we discussed earlier. Identify the man with his work. Here's how Gus Amos does it.

He manages 25 supervisors in the parts installation department of a production company. Each supervisor gets a thorough rundown on the job and his part in getting it done. They write it down so there will be no doubt or excuses. Gus has them report on the work force, tools and paperwork needed, the schedule they will follow, and even how they will maintain housekeeping. He has each supervisor install a sign in the middle of his work area saying, "I am responsible for housekeeping in this area." There is no finger pointing at someone else then, and the men take pride in keeping their own areas as they should be.

Get facilities kept like they ought to be by kindling a man's pride. If he's proud, he'll keep it. A company installed a brand new facility for milling with chemicals. It was the largest and most modern in industry. Each man helped in the design and maintenance of the building and is responsible for his area—they've got pride. Capitalize on a man's pride and help him feel he has the best job in the world. When his work becomes a reason for existence, he'll overwhelm you with good workmanship.

I once passed through a little hamlet of about 100 people. Beside the road was a small, neat luncheonette. I just couldn't make it to the next town of any size, so I stopped for a hamburger and a coke. A lady in an apron did the cooking and running of the place. She took the meat from the refrigerator as if it were fragile, placed it on the grill, hovered over it, pampered it, softly added a slice of tomato and lettuce and placed it on a bun. She served it as if nothing else in the whole world mattered. I never had a better hamburger. Serving me the world's best hamburger seemed to be this lady's calling in life.

Pride's the answer. You've got to stir it up in your employees. A large aerospace firm which analyzed over 100,000 errors that accumulated over a five-year period found that carelessness was the predominent cause. The management in the company decided to institute a company-wide campaign to eliminate the carelessness by appealing to pride of workmanship. A campaign including staff meetings to discuss quality, errors and causes was mounted. This later turned to recognition of good work. Anyone who produced high quality over a certain length of time was recognized. The group talked about such people's work in meetings, placed their pictures on bulletin boards, and in many other ways showed appreciation for good work. After completion of a major aircraft contract the cost of rework was figured and plotted along beside the campaign's length. It was discovered that rework cost per aircraft had decreased from an average of over $140,000 per plane to less than $20,000. The appeal to pride had certainly raised the level of workmanship.

Why not do the same thing in your organization? Emphasize pride and cause your workers to raise their level of workmanship.

## GETTING HIM TO FEEL IT IS HIS OWN SHOP

Once you've kindled his pride, your man will raise his level of workmanship. Let's continue to work on his pride by getting him to feel it is his own area.

Mike Detore, a janitor working an area in the data processing section thinks he owns the area. He makes it shine. Someone once dragged a machine across the floor and left marks. Mike was next seen down on his hands and knees erasing them with a cloth—almost like polishing fine silver. His area always sparkles. Of course it doesn't sparkle any more than he does when you mention it to him. Where does he get this drive? His boss, Joe Sailors, insists on men running their own areas. Joe leaves them alone but he checks to see that they know what they're doing. He has helped this man feel like this is his own territory.

"Mike, when people come here and see a spotless area, they invariably ask me who the janitor is. It reflects your high standards." This sort of conversation between Joe and his men instills pride. He has even stopped while talking with visitors and congratulated the janitor in front of them.

Get results and responsible action from your people by encouraging them to treat the place like they own it. No amount of ordering, explaining, cajoling or threatening can get the honest results that pride does. An old manager in the quality assurance business, Edgar Case, is famous for telling his supervisors, "You run your own cost center and come to me if you need help. Tell me how you'll beat budget and how you'll staff manpower. Tell me your operating procedures." Once he gets his men deeply involved they feel like they turn out better work because they feel like it's their own shop. This works at the hourly level as well as the supervisory level. When a man has a problem, ask him to make the decision as if it were his own company.

Training manager Bob Harrison and one of his men wrestled with the problem of what to do on a project that was being developed for the State Board of Education. There didn't seem to be a right answer. Finally Bob said, "You're in charge of that project. You tell me how you intend to complete the program without going over budget." The man did. Whatever the assignment, let it be his. Give him as much room for decisions as possible and "get him to feel it is his own shop" if you really want action.

## DELVING INTO SOMEONE ELSE'S JOB FOR FUN AND INCREASED ABILITY

You can't sit and operate in a vacuum. As an action-getting manager you must know how your work is tied to that of others: you need to know what the managers around you do. Your people are the same. They can't advance or improve by sitting around doing one thing. Why not encourage them to look around?

Steve James was only 17 when he finished high school and went to work for the Quartermaster Corps at Camp Stewart. He worked in the inventory accounting office. Their job was to keep records of all stock received and dispersed from the warehouses. The twenty people who worked in the stock record section ranged in age from 17 to 50. Some had worked there as long as the Quartermaster Depot had been open. They processed paper and posted numbers day in and day out. Steve was curious about other jobs. Why did the paperwork follow a certain path? Why were back orders posted on page 2? Why did the numbering system proceed in a certain fasion? Where did the work go when it left the office? How was it processed in the warehouse? Exactly how did Jane Wilson keep the perishable accounts from arrival to departure?

In six months the sergeant in charge was transferred and one of the civilians had to take over. Who was put in charge? It was not one of the old hands who only handled routines and didn't know what happened at the next desk: it was the youngster who had taken the time and interest to delve into the other jobs and see what made them tick.

Teach your people to be curious and learn the jobs around them. Your whole operation will benefit in the process.

## CONVINCE HIM THAT HIS JOB IS A MAJOR PART OF HIS LIFE, SO ENJOY IT

If a man gripes about his job, he's in trouble: if he's not happy with his job, he's throwing his life away. Watch your people carefully and see if their work is torture or pleasure.

Dick Rich told a group of 3,000 employees of Rich's Department Store, "Let's think about it: you spend an hour getting to your work, eight hours on the job and an hour getting back home. That's ten hours a day with your job. This is two thirds of the time that you're awake. If you're not thoroughly enjoying what you're doing, just biding your time with the job, waiting for the great day yonder, you're throwing your life away."

If you're unhappy with your job, do one of two things: change your job or change your mind. It is possible to sit down and talk yourself into liking the job. You may have talked yourself into disliking it. It is just as easy to give yourself positive pep talks as negative ones. You've also got to furnish the positives for all of your people.

One man in the office next to me makes a profession of being miserable. He spends the biggest part of his time planning what he's going to do when he retires or remembering what he did in college. As far as his work is concerned now, he hates it. He's just killing time. Instead of enjoying today he's living in the past or in the future. Another reason you should rotate jobs is to increase interest and variety. Any job can get stale after a certain number of years. Why not rearrange the duties so that a man gets some fresh assignments? If a man particularly hates a certain part of his job, maybe it could be given to someone else who would like it.

Employee orientation was the worst assignment in the personnel office. Charles Storch let Tommy Thorbush take it after he seemed interested. Tommy got a lot of satisfaction out of working with the new employees. His planning helped the new employees get better treatment. In the right hands, this unwanted job was handled correctly, and Tommy was happy doing what he enjoyed.

Jake Arrison, a twenty-year employee in a machine shop, commented when someone complimented him on being an authority in his field, "Yeah, and it slipped up on me. I just worked a day at a time and did my best. Time slipped by and I learned more and more. Suddenly, I know the whole works and now I'm an authority. I've spent my whole career on a job I like, and the dividend is that I'm now respected in my trade as a professional."

Let your men know that they are building a profession—that at the end of a period of time they will be able to look back and see all they've done. The major part of their lives is spent on the job: it is your obligation to tell them so. You can help them enjoy it as well.

## LETTING YOUR PEOPLE HELP DEFINE THE SCOPE OF THEIR JOBS FOR LASTING RESULTS

Like problem solving, defining jobs brings out the best in your people. They will outdo themselves. You'll probably have to restrain them. One of the best examples that I've ever seen of job identification was in a personnel records group. Six girls decided that they were going to turn out perfect work. This effort came as a result of emphasis by their manager, Gale Warner, on eliminating errors, and his appeal to employees for ways of doing this. After many meetings looking for ways to improve performance, these girls caught on. They talked about the nature of their work and decided to make improvements in each part of it—not just in accuracy and quality, but also in the amount of work.

While Gale was out of the office, his secretary and several statisticians and department clerks and typists decided to see what they could do to make his job easier. They came up with a plan guaranteeing their work the first time around to eliminate the need for him to check and proofread. They agreed to stamp each paper "Guaranteed perfect by _____" and sign their name. Overtime hours, which had been running 50 to 60 hours per week, was partly made up of rechecking. Payroll additions, jury duty, military deferments, separation letters, management directives, and other publications involve a huge amount of detailed material and checking. Each woman decided to take the individual responsibility for accuracy in her work, in spite of the enormous amount of detail. They approached Gale with their plan and he was quick to say, "Let's try it."

After one week, he stopped in to check on progress. He was amazed to see an empty file drawer where rework was normally kept. At any previous time it would have contained as much as 30 hours of rework.

In addition to getting the work done right the first time, the girls found they were actually enjoying the self-imposed challenge. Some of the improvements included:

- Inquiries, instead of taking several days with typing, checking, re-checking and approving, was now done with a guarantee and released immediately.
- Payroll additions were accomplished without a later auditing operation and guaranteed immediately, saving as much as three manhours per day.
- New employees were checked in and investigated, and records filed and guaranteed in one process. This had previously taken several days.

Gale states that not only have overtime expenditures been reduced, but morale is at its highest peak. Each person is confident in her own ability and feels a responsibility for perfection in her own work. As the girls say, "We used to be defensive about our defects. This caused over-checking. Now that we've analyzed the scope of our jobs, a little extra thought the first time is the secret."

In using all types of motivation ideas, I've never found one that works better than creating job identification. It's almost failure-proof.

## THE EASY WAY TO SET UP MEASUREMENTS

The basic design staff was being rated as a group, but judging each man's work was more difficult. Earl Staddocks, manager, decided to get their help. "How should your work effectiveness be measured?" he asked them. After a series of sessions his men came up with criteria:

- The time factor: the length of time a man works on a basic design. Some engineers will work forever if someone doesn't stop them.
- Completeness of design: lettering, dimensions, designation.
- Neatness.
- References in the design.

The men helped develop these parameters; consequently, they were happy with them. Earl got the criteria set for the jobs, and the men made it work. If you let your men help you define the scope of their jobs you'll get top results from them. You won't have to sweat over setting up criteria either.

## TALKING ABOUT HIS PAST SUCCESSES
## CAUSES HIM TO WANT MORE

It's terribly easy to criticize but harder to compliment. Master the art of recalling the good that a worker does. You can get your men to accept responsibility and really get involved if you remind them of their successes. Don DeLowe needed a manager to conduct a session on production control. Ronnie Maxison had done the job for him twice before. At first Don was afraid he would not want to do it again. Was he imposing? Don waded in and talked about Ronnie's past successes. Visitors were very well pleased with the information in other sessions and had asked pertinent questions as a result of the discussion. "I hate to get off a winner," Don began, "So I'm back again. Can you do it?" Ronnie just beamed. Sure he could: he enjoyed the satisfaction of helping the visitors. He wanted a little more.

The same was true in the case of Vern Haldrop a production troubleshooter. He had represented his organization in several meetings though he felt it was not really his responsibility. However, his manager, Jim Weeks, approached him once more and asked him to attend the meeting. He reminded Vern that in the other meetings he had been able to get results because of his production background and knowledge. Vern was pleased at the chance to repeat his success.

Bill Taylor, who runs a company mail room, can get things done. Anytime anyone wants material traced they call on him. They always say, "You haven't missed yet." This spurs Bill on, as it would anyone. Let your man know you remember every moment of his past successes and encourage him to have them happen again.

Review for a moment the easy ways that you can get involvement and instill responsibility:

- Help the man identify with his job and learn jobs relating to it.
- Show him the importance of customer's feelings.
- Remove some of his mental boundaries and let him run his own shop.
- Tie his work to company objectives.

These are a few of the guidelines that you've just studied. They're restated to help you get real results. Let's consider next how you build checkpoints to be sure the results are there on time.

# 8

## MANAGE SUCCESSFULLY BY USING CHECKPOINTS TO KEEP ACTION ON TARGET

You've broken down the job into components, assigned it to the right man (you hope!), and established a priority with him to get it to you in certain condition at a certain time. Can you now sit back and take a break and celebrate? Well, it's not quite that easy.

Let's take one more step to ensure that you get action on target.

First, build in sufficient checkpoints; then watch the symptoms like a hawk; finally, take corrective action in time.

What do I mean by "checkpoint?" This is the point at which you check in with the performer of a job and see that it is going correctly. A conscientious man will keep you informed and let you know how he stands.

Since such a man is a part of a vanishing breed, you'll need to schedule checkpoints yourself. You've got to make up for any weakness that the performer might have. After all, you'll get the blame if the job doesn't succeed. Help protect your own security: use checkpoints.

Here are some guidelines that will help you use checkpoints successfully to keep the action on target.

1. Require members of your group to report back to you regularly.
2. Determine exactly when you must get back "in the act" and how you'll do it.

3. Watch for symptoms of anyone's failure and adjust your role accordingly.
4. Set a time to follow up and rectify.
5. Expect things to go wrong and take steps far enough ahead of time to correct.
6. Allow extra time in making a deadline assignment.
7. Don't be afraid to use "crutches" to be sure you check assignments at the right time.
8. Develop a foolproof way to remind yourself to follow up.
9. Know when to stop following up.

Let's examine each one separately.

## REQUIRE THE OTHER PERSON TO
## CHECK BACK WITH YOU

Irving Elliott, the chief inspector of a manufacturing company, always builds in checkpoints for inspecting completed assemblies. He knows that there must be many inspections to assure that everything is in place. Suppose his inspectors sat around until a part was completely assembled and sealed up, and then tried to determine the accuracy of what was underneath? The inspectors must determine accuracy ahead of the assembling and sealing.

Elliott stationed several inspectors in Engineering at the beginning of the whole process. After talking with the engineers, these men decided to require that no part can move past a certain point on the line without being inspected. They literally "buy off" the part before it moves along.

This is a checkpoint. Why not do the same in managing other processes? Get the man to check in before he can move to another stage.

## DETERMINE EXACTLY WHEN YOU MUST GET
## BACK IN THE ACT, AND HOW YOU WILL DO IT

The importance of the project and your knowledge of the man will help determine when to "get back in" and to what extent.

- If you have built a critical path so that one step must be done before another, in a certain order, then a missed deadline could hold up the whole process. Such an assignment needs close watching.

  In manufacturing, there is a setback chart or master schedule that shows when small parts for subassemblies and completed assemblies must be completed. Each point on this setback chart has a due date. Production is verified to see that the parts will be ready and will meet at the next point.

  You need to know when the second and later steps in any critical path activity will begin. Verify that the first step is being performed correctly so that it will be completed in time to start the second step.

- If you are training a man, he may need close watching.

  He has to make some mistakes in order to learn. Decide how many mistakes you can tolerate before you must stop him and get him back on the right path. Can you afford to let him ruin a piece of metal? If so, check back when he has completed the first cut. Can you afford to let him ruin two pieces? If so, check back after he has had time to go through the first part. In either case you'll have to grin and bear it while he learns. You have to decide the price to pay and the frequency with which to check back.

- If safety or big money is involved, you may need to watch more closely, depending on your knowledge of the man's capabilities.

- If the company or department's prestige is at stake, keep taking the pulse. A report on Equal Employment Opportunity is due in the vice president's office by Thursday. You made the assignment a week ago and know that your department will look bad if it isn't in on time. Data has to come from three people, be consolidated by a fourth person, typed by a fifth, proofread and then given to you. Be sure that the fourth person has material by Monday; then even if the report goes through typing and proofing and you don't like it, there is time to redo it before the deadline.

There are many ways to get your man to report to you. The project or assignment itself may call attention to an easy way. If not, try one of these:

- On a time basis—"Please report your progress every Friday."
- At an unexpected event—"Let me know if anything goes wrong or you need anything."

- At certain stages—"Whenever you complete Step 1, come back to me and I'll discuss the next step," or "and we'll get supplies for the second step," or "call me and then you can move to the next step."

Whichever basis you use, identify well ahead of time when you expect to hear from him: don't let it be a surprise. If possible, let him have the obligation of reporting back to you.

## REPORTING BACK CAN WORK LONG DISTANCE

A service company contracted with the federal government to send representatives into South American countries to promote civic organization for local progress. Ted Brooks managed these representatives and handled some of the visits himself. He believes in the power of checkpoints.

He visits with a group of the businessmen and discusses civic development, its requirements, how to organize, advantages, etc. How does he guarantee action after he leaves?

He asks them to: (1) appoint a temporary chairman, (2) set a date for an election of their officers, and (3) forward the results to him by a certain date. This last commitment gives him control. He can then proceed with getting a working organization.

You may not ever get an assignment this exotic, but the same principle can work for you in checking work.

## CARBON COPIES SERVE AS A MEANS OF AUDITING TO GET TIMELY CHANGE

The production manager and inspection manager of a company disagreed violently on the requirements of tracking down discrepancies. Finally, Jake Abbott, the industrial engineering manager, did some mediating. Jake had a functional authority over the other two. He got them together and after much discussion, asked George Riley, the production manager, what he would do to straighten out the problem. He said he'd write a memo to supervisors to give notice to the inspection supervisors whenever they wanted a discrepancy traced. They would also enter this in a log.

Jerry Swartz, the inspection manager, reluctantly said he'd write a memo to his supervisors defining the same requirements and asking them to log the inspection date. Jake said, "Great! Send me a copy of each."

A week later Jake had a copy of George's memo, but not Jerry's. All Jake had to do was remind the inspection manager to get his memo out: in two days his copy arrived. Jake would not have noticed the lack of response if he hadn't asked for copies. They provided a means of assuring that the memos were written.

After you have developed a means of getting a man to report back, you still need to make sure that things are in order. Let's look at some of the signs that tell you how the employee is making out.

## WATCH FOR SYMPTOMS OF ANYONE'S FAILURE AND ADJUST YOUR ROLE ACCORDINGLY

My neighbor is good at playing pool. He can recognize other enthusiasts right away. He says, "Note the guy who says, 'I can't really shoot pool very well. I'm just a truck driver on my way through town and want to kill an hour . . .' Watch out! Just by watching this chap select a cue stick you begin to get the picture. If he feels them carefully with his finger tips, that's the start. Watch the way he moves around the table, the way he eyes the table, and the way he eyes you. He'll give himself away."

If that much of a man's action is seen at a pool table, why not in a work situation? Look closely and the other fellow will give you a signal. He'll show you whether or not he is going to get prompt and correct action.

Several expert managers in every kind of organizations from industrial relations to plant engineering were asked how they judge progress on the job. One said, "Intuition." Another answered, "Gut feeling." They agreed that intuition or gut feeling was a summary of years of experience. Here are some specific symptoms to watch for:

- *He's not there.* He starts avoiding you. There are many ways a man can get to his desk and avoid going by the boss's office if he's running late on a job. He can even get tied up by some other "necessary" activities that preclude finishing his own past-due work. Nail him down long enough to get an understanding of what is due when and what the trouble is.
- *He's defensive.* If a few prying questions get you defensive answers or

excuses, you've surely got trouble. When he makes statements like "You didn't say you wanted it in final form," or "Why did you let John come in and rewrite the first two paragraphs?" or "I can't possibly finish it on time if Ralph doesn't try to cooperate," stop and see how the job stands.

- *He makes excuses.* He may say "I'm getting all kinds of delays from photography," or "They won't set aside computer time," or "Jack just put me on special assignment." If he doesn't work for you, watch signs like, "My boss is harassing me about this other project." It could mean yours is going to pot. Get to his boss or whomever necessary to get it back on track.
- *He's fiddling around.* If the man wastes time getting started or makes false starts, he might not understand the assignment or have materials. Better check him out again.
- *He doesn't seem to care about due date.* "Well, I've got to get it right regardless of the time it takes." If he hasn't concerned himself about when it's due, how can he deliver on time?
- *He shows little volume of work.* Some jobs—typing, art, calculations, etc.—require certain amounts of output. There should be visual evidence of these. Start reviewing if output is not in view.
- *He's sick.* Some employees feel that sickness is unquestionable even at the sacrifice of a due date. An uncomfortable assignment can cause him to look for a way out. I know a man who gets "stomach poisoning" regularly. It is really a delay in performance or just a bid for attention. Prescription: Do a little extra checking on the status of his work.

These signs are not foolproof, but each could provide room for suspicions. The successful manager is a suspicious manager, although he might not show it in front of his people. If he is observant, he can set and read his own catalogue of symptoms.

### IF HE MISSES INSTRUCTIONS, DETAILS, OR GIVES INDIRECT OR GENERALIZED ANSWERS, STEP IN AND DEAL WITH THE PROBLEM

Consider these situations where the manager saved the day by reading the symptoms:

- *The man misses instructions.* Three visitors arrived to spend a few months studying production and procurement systems in an industry.

Jay Tuell, the public relations manager, had the responsibility of overseeing their stay. He had done this before and was ready for anything.

Two of the visitors were right on target, but D. G. Parsons, the other, kept missing his cues. On the second day he forgot his pass. Four days later he forgot it again. A short while later, when the men were getting ready to visit an area where coats are usually worn, Parsons left his in the car.

A week later, Parsons arrived in an office and asked, "Where did everyone go?" They went where they were supposed to go, clear across the plant to another office that they had agreed on the day before. The symptoms of Parsons' unconcern were stacking up.

Jay got the picture pretty quickly and began double-checking to assure that during the rest of Parson's stay he arrived on time and in the right place.

- *The man misses details.* Bob Harrison manages training in the Value Engineering Company. He has a group of coordinators that handle specific assignments. Some are better than others. One coordinator, Jim Garner, "fed in" symptoms of trouble until Bob finally had to take action.

Jim walked into the classroom packed with students and waited for the instructor. The instructor didn't show. A phone call showed he was out of town and knew nothing about the class. Jim had reserved the room, notified departments to send students and had done many other things, but he failed to notify the instructor.

Checking showed that this had happened on other occasions. One time a teacher arrived and the class didn't. Another time they all arrived and the room wasn't available. Jim just couldn't be trusted on details. He'd been warned; he'd promised to do better; he does other things well, but he just can't handle details. Bob finally took several steps to make up for this weakness. He gave Jim a checklist on which Jim must enter the dates that he arranged for a room, called the instructor, ordered supplies, etc. The arrangements are now staying on track. After using this routine many times, Jim developed the habit of following through without physically having the checklist.

- *The man won't give a direct answer.* The public relations manager, Jay Tuell, had to arrange a speaker for a conference and asked for help from a friend, Al Meade. Al knew the proposed speaker, Lloyd Jason. "I'll try," Al replied, "But he is terribly busy and I don't have much hope." He reported back later, "Jason will be in Canada at the time of your conference."

"If we have the conference in May, could he come then?" Jay asked.

"I don't know, I'll see."

Weeks later, "He's terribly busy. It doesn't look like he can come."

"Have you actually asked him?"

"Well, er, ah, no. I talked to some of his friends."

"Please ask him."

Days later Al reported, "He'll be here. In fact, he's delighted to come."

Al almost missed getting Jason for the conference, because he didn't actually ask him. Al isn't an action-getter. Fortunately Jay spotted this in his conversation; he was suspicious and kept insisting until action was taken.

*The man talks in generalities.* A safety program in the Ajax Trucking Company was assigned to Don Jewell. Bill Rowe had had enough experience with Don to know how to check on his progress. He asked Don one day, "How are you going to handle details within the Finance Department?"

Don replied, "I'll tie them in later." He also stated, "We'll check the employees out on safety practices."

Checking further, Bill still found Don's plans indefinite. Don's remark "Safe conditions will be provided in the storage area," proved to be more a wish than a plan. Rowe immediately made Don define each step of his plan and show how he would implement it. He had long since learned that generalities can cover a lot of ground, some of which might not have been plowed.

## LISTEN TO CASUAL COMMENTS THAT CAN INDICATE WHAT IS HAPPENING

The project was under control, or so the boss, Harry McCoy, thought. In three weeks a proposal for Job Corps training was supposed to be delivered to Washington. McCoy had put Pat Crawley in charge: he wouldn't let any grass grow under his feet. Yet an alert typist stated quite casually one day, "No one is giving me any rough notes on the project to type."

In another conversation one of the rewrite men commented, "I haven't seen any of the drafts that need rewriting." At this point, if things were on schedule, there should have been material. McCoy immediately called a status meeting with the project director, Crawley. Sure enough, the timing was off. McCoy put out extra effort and got the project back on schedule.

## PUT ALL YOUR SENSES TO WORK TO SEE ACTION IS ON THE RIGHT TRACK

Words and actions alone often don't show us all the symptoms. There are other good means of finding them.

Walt Johnson, a manager at Jenkins Sheet Metal, tells his men to learn how to "walk" the job. He means that as his men walk in an area where employees are working, they should listen for the sound of a drill that is entering the metal wrong. It has a definite ring or hum when it goes in straight and another when it goes in crooked. He also states that the chemicals smell a certain way when fresh and another way when stale. Touching the metal in some instances can reveal softness that should not be there.

## GET CORRECTIVE ACTION WHILE THERE IS STILL TIME FOR SUCCESSFUL COMPLETION

If you've built in adequate checkpoints and you are watching every symptom to see how things are going, then you can take corrective action soon enough.

An item was mailed to Montreal for an important meeting two weeks later. It had to clear customs, which was done locally. What could possibly go wrong? It was sent by Air Mail two weeks early.

Doc Wilson, the manager, always anticipated trouble. He told the Montreal representative to call him the following Wednesday if the item had not arrived. On Wednesday Doc got a call from Montreal.

The item had apparently not gone by Air Mail after all. A duplicate item was dispatched by Air Mail and arrived on time. The manager's instruction to call a week before due date was the safeguard which saved the day.

Regardless of the checkpoints that you have built in, there is no rest for the diligent action-getter. Anticipate trouble and you'll be ready for it.

## SET A TIME TO FOLLOW-UP AND RECTIFY

As an action-oriented manager, only one thing satisfies you: results. You can't be satisfied with less just because your own name is clear.

Corrective action while there was still time could have avoided embarrassment in this case:

> Over a six-month span, the supplies department in a business college was asked to order material from an outside source for three classes. The supplies were to be shipped a few days before each class.
>
> —For the first class, the material arrived on time.
> —For the second, no material arrived. The supplies department called at the last minute and the shipment was delivered.
> —Last class, again, no material. Supplies called at the last minute, but the material still did not arrive in time for the class.
>
> The supplies manager immediately stated, "It wasn't our fault. We told them what was needed." But did they follow up before it was too late? No one even kept a reminder. That's a good example of how not to get results.

When a mistake becomes history nothing can change it. Hiding behind "I did what I was supposed to" won't replace results. There is absolutely no excuse acceptable when the goal is not accomplished. Remember, your goal is to get results.

## EXPECT THINGS TO GO WRONG AND TAKE
## STEPS FAR ENOUGH AHEAD TO CORRECT THEM

A major reason for follow-up is to make corrections that lead to successful action. If you don't leave time to make the corrections, why embarrass yourself by finding something wrong and just suffering through it?

Rick Sims worked with a local restaurant to set up a banquet for a graduating group of apprentices. The banquet was scheduled to take place the following evening at 6:30 p.m.

Rick told his manager, "I think I'll leave tomorrow around 4:30 to get there in time to see that everything is all right."

Henry Turner, his manager, replied, "If you expect to correct something, go while you've got time." The manager had learned this through experience.

So Rick went at 3:00 p.m. and found the program badly planned, sound equipment not in order, no arrangements made for serving part of the food, and numerous other things to be corrected. Fortunately there was still time to get arrangements made and have the program succeed.

### FUDGE A LITTLE IN MAKING A DEADLINE ASSIGNMENT TO ALLOW EXTRA TIME

Give yourself a few extra days in setting a deadline: then in an absolute emergency you've got a little "give." (For example, if you need a report by March 8, ask that it be completed by March 6.) If you do this too often, however, your people will suspect and start taking up the slack themselves.

Jim's manager asked him to publicize a safety problem in the Paint Shop. Jim turned to Mack Simpson, the manager of the art department, for advice. Mack recommended these steps:

—Get some rough ideas and take them to an artist for sketches.
—Get the manager to approve the idea.
—Find out the number of copies needed to cover all employees.
—Get the final sketch approved and deliver it to Printing.
—Printing delivers back to Jim for distribution.

Everything seemed to move along until Mack realized, two days before distribution time, that the copies hadn't arrived.

"Haven't they had time to arrive?" Mack asked.

"Come to think of it, yes," was Jim's answer.

"Better call Printing and check it out."

The call proved they hadn't been sent. In fact, they were sitting in the corner gathering dust. Fortunately Mack had dealt with enough similar situations to know when to check.

## DON'T BE AFRAID TO USE "CRUTCHES" TO BE SURE YOU CHECK ASSIGNMENTS AT THE RIGHT TIME

In order to correct in time, of course, you'd better know what time element is involved. Most of us have to use memory joggers and checkpoints.

It's better to cushion a poor memory than let the assignment disintegrate. There are many crutches and follow-up systems that successful managers use.

Try one of these reminders for following up to get corrective action on time:

One system is composed of standard file folders, numbered 1 through 31 for the days of the month. Into these folders you should put notes, booklets, letters, or any other form of reminder of a particular item that you need for checking action on a date in the future. First thing in the morning, pull out the folder for that day and remove the pending notes; then put the folder back in sequence.

An old standby is the calendar on which you can write notes of pending action. The standard desk calendar is almost always used for this purpose. Write everything on it that will get action when you need it. In addition, a calendar showing one month on a single page is fine for keeping track of trips, obligations, speaking engagements, etc. This is ideal when you need to see at a glance the action that should take place in any particular month. It can be filed later as a record.

One manager uses a little book of items that need to be done in which he puts down the action taken, leaving the final column open until he has the results. He can check at any particular time, look at the open items, and know whether or not he's got things pending that he needs to take action on. There's a memo pad that fits in your coat pocket for just such a purpose.

## DEVELOP A FOOLPROOF WAY TO REMIND YOURSELF TO FOLLOW UP

Here are some other reminders:

Some managers are chart-happy. One I know has a room with every wall covered. He can check the progress of any item that is being purchased anywhere in the industry. He can tell you just where any bog-down is right to the very cost center and group that is causing it. Maybe we ought to look twice at charts. As long as it isn't only kept to look good to top brass and give coordinators something to do, a progress chart can be a handy reference point and memory jogger.

Another advantage of charting is that it makes it pretty hard for anyone else on your staff to miss the fact that you are keeping close tabs. If you have several assignments going simultaneously you can post them all on the chart with due date or ECD (earliest completion date). There's no reminder better than the visual one.

A busy supervisor in an inspection department sits down each morning and lists all pending items and tasks he must account for during the day, checking them off as they are completed.

A secretary puts a gem clip on the calendar if a message comes through when she can't mark the calendar. A few minutes later she removes the gem clip and makes notes. A good secretary is the best possible reminder—just be sure and tell her what you want to remember.

Try putting something in an unusual place to remind yourself. A wallet removed from the normal hip pocket and placed in the other will remind you later of an item you wanted to do, but couldn't write down at the moment. This gimmick really works.

Requiring that a man check with you at a specific time, as discussed earlier, is still the best way of getting feedback when needed.

You may have your own system developed. What it is isn't of great importance. What is important is that you take steps to be sure a job is progressing correctly: the steps must be taken when there is still time to adjust the rest of the action. Your objective is still to deliver the goods in good shape, within cost, and on time. This is one of the primary gages that shows that you are a successful manager.

## KNOW WHEN TO STOP FOLLOWING UP

Whatever you do, don't breathe down your man's neck until it's really necessary. You can ask a person to report with such frequency that you overburden him, kill precious time, and take away his initiative.

A former manager thrived on reports and check points. He had several supervisors and administrators reporting to him in the personnel department of a large company. He was very new to management however, and his ego required him to be in the middle of everything. A simple assignment became complex because he required excessive reporting. A straightforward question to him precipitated a conference and reports. In general, his whole style handicapped his people to the point of doubling or tripling their work. He used little discretion in reading symptoms for building checkpoints. Fortunately, his style has long since sent him down the drain and his men are now doubling their production.

Be careful that your checkpoints don't get out of control.

Another man just couldn't stop following up. Follow-up needs to be handed out in just the right doses. Look at his style:

The secretary, the boss and three departments were alerted; two supervisors and three organizations became involved; then, each was called several times and asked, "Is this item being done?"

A man from a consulting company whose assignment was to get a report on morale within several fabrication departments in a production company caused this harassment. He completely demoralized every person in the chain by overcoordinating. He didn't get action—he got mayhem. The results were out on time, but every participant hated him and each other. The next time he'll find the door shut. The smart guy gages the amount of follow-up needed and doesn't overdo it.

Follow-up is like salt in the stew: it's flat with too little, but unbearable with too much.

In summary, take one more step to assure that you get action on target:

—Build in sufficient checkpoints.
—Watch the symptoms like a hawk.
—Take corrective action in time.

# 9

## HOW TO USE FEEDBACK TO GET SHORT-RUN ACTION AND LONG-RUN IMPROVEMENT

The job has got to get out but you've still got to live with your man —or do you? Are you after action only this time around, or are you out to improve your worker? Sometimes it's easy to say "If I get this done I'll close the door and go to another supplier if I have to." It's not so easy to say "I'll chew this fellow out to get the job done, then hire and train another worker. Feedback needs to be considered in light of your next move or your final goal.

Ron Taylor owns a lingerie shop. He has a manager, Clark Gilbert, that he dearly respects for certain traits and could shoot because of others. He has wrestled long with the issue of improvement vs. non-improvement—and he's geared his feedback accordingly. For instance he has discovered that Clark is basically a sloppy person. He leaves materials and half-finished jobs around the store in order to stop and wait on a customer. He handles buying but is lax in considering accounts payable, making Ron retain the strings of finance. Ron has had to analyze what can be changed and what can't. He has reminded Clark about store cleanliness many times—it improves a little, but then gets sloppy again. Ron discovered that Clark is only going to do so much cleanup and that he'll only alienate Clark if he keeps hounding him. After all, Ron says, it is a small price to pay for Clark's other traits.

Ron is making progress with him in the financial situation. He's found a way to let Clark get his own feedback on buying habits and results by setting up a simple bookkeeping system and having Clark handle all the bills. It's working: Clark turned to Ron one day and said, "Hey, Ron, we're in trouble with our buying. We're over-buying XYZ merchandise and not selling enough of it to make it pay for itself." Ron responded, "I'm glad you're getting the message." Clark has improved his buying 100 percent since he started the bookwork and is on the way to making a profit. Joe did it by placing him in the middle of the feedback on his purchasing habits.

Our energy is often devoted to getting long-range improvement in order to develop a good team and get the best group results. However, let's consider aids in getting both the best short-run and long-run action.

### ADVISING A MAN HOW HE'S DOING ON AN ASSIGNMENT SO HE CAN COMPLETE IT SATISFACTORILY

If the man's fairly new, or the assignment vitally important, or both, he needs to know that he is on the right track. As an astute manager you must be able to give all the needed information on a moment's notice or be able to call on the man who can.

Ray Stanton was appointed the head of an assembly-line corrective action committee made up of representatives of numerous affected organizations trying to iron out production problems. Pat Patterson, manager of one of the projects involved, wasn't actually on the committee, but was concerned about results which would affect his project. He was also concerned about production and the success of the various managers. Pat saw trouble coming for Ray since his system was bogging down even before it started. For example, Ray was keeping too many records and not keeping the necessary people informed about his team's progress. He was also not taking a strong role in leading the men who had been assigned to him.

Pat was close enough to the problem to see these things. He had a long talk with Ray, advising him to take corrective action within his own committee before it got out of hand by changing the reporting and record-keeping systems. He advised Ray to see that his men had strong assignments within the group and total accountability. Ray knew of Pat's earnest concern and wisdom, so he listened.

The Corrective Action Committee flourished and Ray received praises from several dozen managers. He thanked Pat for taking the time to help him get on the right track. Pat got satisfaction in knowing that he had helped avoid a mess.

You should be constantly attuned to your man's progress. The systems of checkpoints that we discussed in the last chapter can give you the input. Move in when necessary and help the man with any information that will help him to complete the assignment successfully and add to your stature as an action-getting manager.

### HOW TO GIVE UNFAVORABLE FEEDBACK
### AND STILL MOTIVATE FOR IMPROVEMENT

Criticism is easy to give. It takes a little more wisdom to get someone to operate in the face of it. It can sometimes be very demoralizing.

Twenty-two years ago when I started teaching managers to speak in front of groups, I learned a lesson. Almost everyone in the class said, "Tell me what I'm doing wrong." They never came back to class when I did. Finally it dawned on me that they really wanted to know that there was hope—that they weren't all bad and could learn to speak. So I started looking for other ways to get improvement. I soon found that you can give unfavorable feedback and still motivate, but it takes extra thought.

Everyone is looking for a feeling of importance, recognition or appreciation. When you say to someone who's working, "Hey, Buddy, you're messing that up," he's not even close to getting that thing he's looking for. You can understand why he rationalizes, excuses, lies, or does anything else to justify himself. You're swimming upstream. The one thing he doesn't say is, "That's just what I've been waiting to hear."

If we accept that philosophy, we can find an approach that won't wound his ego but make him want to improve.

It reminds me of Sharky Ward, an accounts payable manager, who was asked to use one rule all week and report on it. The rule was

"Help the other person feel important." We already stated that if a manager couldn't find something in a person's performance to praise, that the manager needed to polish his sights. Sharky related this story.

"When Sam Durham brought in his report, it was poorly written: it had many inaccurate figures, and was in generally bad shape. I remembered the rule I was to use and tried to think of something I could say that would honestly help this fellow feel important about something that he did well. I was almost ready to give up when it dawned on me: Sam always has his report in on time. I said, 'Sam, you are one of the few in the whole office who gets his report in on time.' With that you should have seen Sam beam. *It was not flattery* either; it was true. Then I said, 'Now, Sam let's see if we can get these figures straightened out.' Sam was anxious to improve and started showing up with better reports each time. It was easier to work with him because he was receptive."

We can use the same principles that Sharky used and get improvement. Cushion unfavorable feedback with more acceptable information. Of course this idea can be overdone if you don't use a little common sense. One manager in a purchasing office was known as a hypocrite because he opens with a compliment and then jabs his men with a sharp rebuke. The idea, rather, is to honestly let the man see his need for change in relation to some of his better points. That way criticism is not so hard to take.

As a manager, you must get change or you'll flunk. This idea will help you get it. Keep the worker motivated while you suggest improvements.

### HOW TO TAKE THE STING OUT OF "CONSTRUCTIVE" CRITICISM

You and I never criticized anyone in our lives except constructively—in our own minds at least. We've all said: "After all, we are doing it for his own good." "We are managers and are supposed to." "He needs correcting in order to do the job right." "He ought to be big enough to take it." There is another criteria that is far more important however. The key factor is not that we give criticism constructively, but that the other fellow receive it constructively.

Do you know the difference between criticism and "constructive" criticism? If I criticize you, it's "constructive," but if you criticize me, then it's plain old criticism. The real test is how it is being received.

You can remove the sting by setting your own mind right first or by cushioning it with some positive comment such as, "John, you are getting the outline great, now let's see if we can improve the lettering."

You may remove the sting by watching your language. We mentioned earlier that words have stigma. In no case is this truer than when it applies to an individual. It's far easier to accept that something "can be improved" than to accept that it is "wrong," "botched," "fouled up," or "poor."

Remove the sting by criticizing the job rather than the individual. Don't let him feel that he is under attack if it is only the job that's wrong. "This particular item needs _____." "Jake, you usually get the layout right, this edge needs sharpening."

Keep in mind that no matter how good our intentions, criticism is likely to have a more venomous sting than we intend. Use any of these ideas to help remove that sting.

## AVOIDING CRITICAL COMMENTS THAT WON'T HELP HIM IMPROVE

If you've got a flood of criticism for the man, don't let it all pour out at once. Even if he breaks other company rules or has other sins, your purpose is to get a certain job—stick with it. Unless you're given an overall appraisal, stick to the subject. For some reason, one negative comment tends to lead to another.

It will be hard enough for him to take a little criticism without being inundated with it. Bonnell Craven, the craft store manager, has had her share of problems getting instructors for craft courses.

Lou Baker, one of her instructors, was a prima donna, but a fine instructor. Once she let her students pour paint down the toilet, stopping it up. Lou also had let them use easels without buying them and complained about the brushes. Lou was really going out of her way to teach the class, but there had to be rules. Fortunately Bonnell knows Lou well enough to know how to handle her. Instead of talking about all of the problems at once, Bonnell took only one that stands out. She started with the brushes, telling Lou that she needs to help sell the store's equipment, rather than picking it apart, since that is where the money was made. When she approached all of this calmly, Lou agreed. Later that day, when Bonnell said, "Oh, by the way Lou, how about reminding your students to pour their paints out back rather than down the drain," Lou said, "Sure."

Bonnell had resisted the urge to move in with all critical remarks at one time. She also resisted telling Lou that she needed to think of the store. When she made only the necessary criticism in the right tone she got improvement and kept a good instructor.

One manager started out discussing a supervisor's slowness on a certain job and progressed to talking about the fact that he didn't get along with the other supervisors. From there he went into a long harangue about the man's inability to get along with people. The flood gate opened and this manager trapped himself in the inevitable deluge.

Manage an interview as well as you manage your people. Say only what you want to say. Hold back any criticism that won't help.

## SETTING THE SCENE FOR SUCCESSFUL RECEPTION

When you correct a man it should be:

—Not in front of others, please.
—When he's not emotionally upset.
—When you're not emotionally upset.
—When there are no interruptions or distractions.

This may not be as necessary in simple corrections, but it certainly is if you are going to give him any sort of in-depth appraisal or suggestions.

I sat in my office one day and watched while others marched in and out of the office next to me. It was usually reserved for a colonel who's head of the Air Force team visiting on projects. The people that were using it were members of the technical research department. Each one went in with John Seymore who was giving appraisals. He had refused to talk with his people unless he could put them in a quiet office and shut out interruptions. Consequently his appraisals were well received, and he avoided poor reception.

Set the scene physically as John did; then set it mentally by letting the man know why you are talking. If it is one project that needs discussing, get on with it. If it is his whole performance, let him know that it is time to take a look at his future. Let him realize the feedback is for his growth and improvement and not just a whim of management. You'll sustain long-range results.

## CONDITIONING A MAN TO EXPECT FEEDBACK IN ORDER TO IMPROVE

Start early. When I first went to work with a manufacturing firm, I was given absolute freedom and very little instruction in planning my work—until I did something wrong. Then I got it. It was really devastating.

A much better plan is to take a man through his work or assignments telling him what you feel is necessary, how you are going to appraise him and when:

If it is during and at the end of each assignment,
If it is going to be every six months, regardless of assignments, or
If it is going to be a combination of these.

He really should know how to expect feedback.

The best feedback is that which comes constantly and unpretentiously, as an everyday part of the job. You may have too many men or too many assignments to keep this pace: that is one reason for scheduling yourself and him so you will be held to certain minimums.

Security manager Dale Hopkins took a new man into his department. The guards were constantly in the public eye serving over 25,000 employees. They had to deal effectively with people, know the plant and be able to work under all kinds of conditions. Dale had a long chat with the man, Burt Paschal, defining the criteria for good performance. He went over dress, manners and the behavioral standards. More importantly, he told the man that he'd like to talk with him in a week and see how he was doing. When he did, Burt was missing part of his uniform, but Dale got him on track. The man has had little trouble, so Dale has continued to give him feedback periodically. Now Burt is shaping up well, fulfilling Dale's expectations.

In Dale's case there was no particular assignment, but a constant ongoing performance that needed feedback. That's the hardest kind of schedule: it's easier to include a review at the end of any assignment.

Ed Pleek does this with all of his process engineers. As a man finishes an assignment Ed has a checkout man go over everything with the individual. The man gages his quality immediately. Ed then goes over the man's whole performance with him every few months. This keeps his men working at their best.

Set a pattern with your men early and often so that they can make any changes for short-run or long-run improvement.

## GIVING AN OVERALL APPRAISAL PERIODICALLY
## TO KEEP TOTAL PERFORMANCE UP

I once heard a manager say, "I don't need to give appraisals. My men know where they stand at all times." It isn't always that way, especially in a large company. The larger the department or group, the greater the trouble and the need can be.

Ideally we should keep a man knowledgeable of how he's doing at all times. There also needs to be documentation for future reference. Suppose the manager in a large company quits? A man could have been working for him five years without there being any record of how the man was doing. When a new manager comes in, he might have to start over evaluating his men's abilities.

I'm not completely in favor of written appraisals, although I've given my share in my time. It bothers me to subject another man to *my* standards, *my* evaluation, and *my* feedback. I might be a miserable manager with ridiculous standards, sticking the man with my rating. However, a poor appraisal is still better than nothing on file.

We could devote a whole book to appraisals—many have—but we still wouldn't lick some of the major problems. Let's accept the problems and take a look at how we can do the best job of letting him know where he stands while leaving documentation for the future.

How is he doing in relation to:

—Preset standards?

—Other workers?

—His potential?

*Preset standards:* This means checking him off on individual projects. How well is he hitting your requirements for quality, cost, and schedule, and also special behavioral standards? Check each job, making notes to file in his folder. If he accomplishes a major project that's up to your standards, why not write it down? Is he consistently missing schedule? Your work is cut out for you here. Is he oblivious to costs? Is there some other factor that he keeps missing? If so, you need to talk to him.

Saul Lamert supervises a production line group. Its rapid-fire action and need for fast decisions are really a testing ground of managerial ability. Saul has 13 men working for him and usually has half a dozen separate projects running simultaneously. He has a sharp eye, but still spends a tremendous amount of time seeing how his men are doing. To be absolutely sure he doesn't miss a trick, he checks out each assignment from a book. As the assignment is completed, he makes performance notes by his men's names. This only takes a few more minutes but gives him a sound basis for evaluating each man's total performance and the group's accomplishment. Saul has received several commendations from his manager for his ability to make near-perfect assignments. This has resulted from his ability to appraise each man's ability and assign accordingly.

*Other Workers:* If six other workers do a certain kind of work right and one doesn't, then that one has a problem. If they all miss, then there's a problem with your standards. It is almost impossible to have a group working without comparing each man to the rest. This isn't necessarily bad. It gives you a gage of his ability. Be sure he isn't being overmatched, however. He'll be miserable and so will you. Get him in a group where he can work.

One of Saul's men had to be transferred. Saul put him to work cutting a patch out of an aluminum siding. The man, call him Sam, had a devil of a time doing it. He drilled a hole in the wrong place and had to have it covered. He elongated holes and had to have them riveted. Saul put him to work on another project that could be repaired more easily. Sam did about the same. Saul tried him next on layout and found he could do that well. Since none of the others in the group had any trouble with patching, Saul decided that Sam would be better off in the layout organization, so he transferred him to another department. After that Sam had very little trouble. It becomes necessary every so often to look at how the man is making out in relation to the other workers.

*His Potential:* If you had a fleet of psychologists to do all the work, this might be easier. They could run voluminous tests, rate people and do all the things they are famous for. Let's assume you don't have that big team in front of you and have looked at your man's potential yourself.

There isn't any easy way to know his potential without just plain knowing the man. Watch every bit of his progress. If he shows ability in writing, try him on it. If he shows ability in follow-up, give him more of that to do. If he shows ability in dealing with people, make him "straw boss" over a project. Find some way to try out every indication of latent talent. Your shrewd eye is the best test of what he's got.

In a Coast Guard recruiting school held monthly in New York City, recruiters are evaluated on how well informed they are about the Coast Guard, how well they present speeches, and how they answer questions on a quiz. But above all else, they are rated on how well they participate in class and relate to other people. How do they appear? How do they sell themselves? These latter questions are terribly hard to answer on paper, but are often the most necessary.

In your case, you'll help the man most by using your own powers of observation to help analyze his potential.

## HOW TO LISTEN AND LEARN
## EVEN IN GIVING FEEDBACK

Many managers listen with their mouths. Creative listening, like creative managing or selling, is an art. It involves knowing how to ask questions that get the best information from your man, and allowing him to get any of his concerns out in the open.

If a kettle is boiling and the steam is escaping all is well, but if you put a cap on the spout, the lid will fly off. Cap the lid and it'll explode. You want to let a man give you any of his concerns or his thinking so that it's out in the open.

It can be hard to let the other man talk, when you've started with something on your mind that you want to tell him. You should run the conversation, but let him talk too. When you are ready to take over, take over.

"Open" questions give you a chance to understand his real thinking or get him involved in your conversation. Open questions are ones that can't be answered with simply a "yes" or "no" answer. They require at least some degree of thought.

"How did you have trouble with this part?"
"What did you do to get this answer?"
"How will you correct this junction?"
"When did you give the material to Metal Bonding?"
"Tell me the process you went through to get this."

All of these questions require thought.

Once I gave dictation while filling in for a shorthand teacher. I had to speak 120 words a minute for the students. When they could write that fast, I'd move up to 140 words a minute. With Steno-type I'd do up to 180 and 200 words per minute so they'd really have to push. In the process I discovered that I couldn't come close to talking as rapidly as they could take down the words and if they had not had to write they could have listened even faster. People listen many times faster than we speak. We have to force ourselves to listen attentively. I'll restate:

1. Ask open questions to understand some of your employee's thinking.
2. *Make* yourself listen attentively to your employee when you are counseling.
3. Use the information to help him improve.

Chuck Langendoen kept hearing that Sue Ellen Pratt wasn't doing her best in his production control group. Sue Ellen argued with some of the other managers on occasions and made nagging comments to some of her co-workers. Chuck decided that it was time to talk with her about the problem. He called her in and casually asked, "Sue Ellen, how are you doing with your job?" He got a short answer,

"All right, I guess." Chuck sensed that something wasn't right. "How do you like working with the others in this group?" "Well, I guess they're all right." Chuck knew something was wrong and continued, "Sue Ellen, what is it that you don't like about your job?" With this he got a torrent of emotion, "I just hate it," she said. "I've been thinking about quitting. I can't stand to be constantly faced with these shortage problems, unhappy managers and things that are always wrong. It's that way day in and day out. I hate it." It began to dawn on Chuck that he had made a grievous error. He had put Sue Ellen in a critical spot and caused her to face the one kind of work that made her suffer worse than any other. "Sue Ellen, how would you like to work in the blueprint crib?" "I'd love to try it," she replied. She hasn't had a minute's trouble in the new job. Even though it is hectic, it doesn't involve one crisis after another. Chuck has saved a very valuable worker who might have quit if he had not intervened. He was smart enough to recognize symptoms that something wasn't right. Give your employees a chance to air any grievance before giving them feedback, particularly the unfavorable kind.

## CHOOSING THE RIGHT TIME CAN BE HALF THE BATTLE

We'll state it again:

—Not when he's emotionally upset,
—Not when you're emotionally upset, and if possible
—Not when he has been receiving bad feedback all along,
—When the work is fresh in his mind,
—Before he gets into another job,
—When you have plenty of time to handle any turn of the interview.

Another right time is when you are not in front of someone else. Nothing is more inappropriate than to chew out an employee in a meeting or fail to do what you can to stay on his side. I've heard bosses disclaim any part of a wrong action and allow their employees to take full blame in a meeting. Bosses are often at least partly to blame in such cases.

Ed Eiche, an office services manager, missed a golden chance to chew out an employee in a meeting and at the same time proved how shrewd he was. His man Clay Powell was running the meeting, a gathering of group supervisors considering a plan for improving their management selection techniques. Clay was chairman and Ed was sitting in as a high-level visitor. Clay discussed a plan he had evolved. It was a bad plan, but few of the supervisors liked it. Clay turned to Ed and asked, "What do you think?"

"It could probably be improved," Ed stated.

Whereupon Clay blew his stack and said a few heated words.

Ed merely said, "Let's discuss it later. Why don't you go ahead with the meeting?"

Later Ed sat down and politely chastised Clay for losing his cool. He also discussed the plan and how it could be improved. Clay was now under control and saw the point. Ed chose the right time to talk to Ed—when he was calmed down and away from the meeting. That's why Ed is noted as a smart manager. Choosing the right time to criticize is half of the battle for improvement.

## HOW TO BE SPECIFIC IN DEFINING
## ADDITIONAL NEEDS TO IMPROVE

How much more must he do to complete the job? How much better does it have to be? Requirements must be specific if we expect the best improvement of a man.

Another example from Ed Eiche concerns his secretary, Helen Ball. She missed just a little on many assignments. Ed finally decided it was time to dramatize to her that a miss was as good as a mile.

Helen set up a speaking engagement for Ed in the company theater. Ed's office was on the third floor of one building and the theater was in the basement of another building a block away. Helen keeps his calendar and supposedly keeps him out of trouble. She told him on the intercom, "It is time to leave for the meeting." It was then 1:55 and the meeting was at 2:00. When Ed came back later he was disgusted.

"How long does it take to walk to the theater?" he asked Helen.

"Certainly not more than five minutes," she replied.

"Tell you what you do. You leave right now and I'll time how long it takes you to get there and back and then we'll know."

She was aggravated at having to do it, but knew he was terribly annoyed, so she did. When she returned, she learned that it had taken almost 12 minutes each way. He had certainly arrived late for the program.

"Don't guess that closely on timing," he urged her. "Either know or allow more time."

She got the point started working on improving her timing.

You need to ensure that your employee gets the exact message you're sending. Be specific and, if necessary, use drama, as Ed did.

### GETTING HIM TO HELP DEFINE THE NEED FOR IMPROVEMENT WILL MAKE IT ACCEPTABLE

"How do you think it went, Joe?"

"What were you aiming at?"

"If you had it to do over, what would you do differently?"

Let him tell you how it could be improved. The biggest concern is that he'll go overboard! Usually a man will go further in telling his faults if there is no apparent threat than he will if someone else is criticizing him.

Bob Harrison, the training manager, is a master of appraisal. He lets the man fill out his own appraisal and justify it:

—"How do you rate yourself on use of time?"

—"On ability to get along with others?"

—"Ability to carry out instructions?"

He gets a man to rate himself on each count—average, superior or below average—and then in some cases raises the rating or lowers it. In either case he lets the man see why. The only danger is that when you have to lower a rating you may create resentment, so play it carefully. It's worth the gamble in order to get his overall involvement.

After a training session, Bob will ask an instructor, "How do you think they responded? Did they really get the major points? Will they put them in practice? How can you do it better?" This puts the monkey on the instructor's back and makes it easy for him to offer suggestions to himself.

## MAKING SURE YOU KNOW THE FACTS SO
## THAT YOU'LL BE ON SOUND FOOTING

The cardinal sin of management is walking into any situation half cocked. It can't be more dangerous than when you're trying to get improvement. Know the facts! Remember Joe Marr? He had a nasty situation in progress on the production floor. His man, Bill, had managed to antagonize several workers and trapped Joe in the middle of the act. Joe was smart enough to say he'd get back later. He went to the office with Bill to work on the facts. Sure enough Bill was wrong. This allowed Joe to break it to the workers later when they had cooled down and he knew the exact story. Joe avoided getting in over his head by getting the facts.

No manager worth his salt would base a decision on hearsay, nor would he judge an employee on somebody else's information. Get the facts.

L. B. Taylor is assistant manager of an electric company. He listened one day as an employee, Tom Drake, explained his problem. Tom had gone past his supervisor in discussing the problem with L. B. The supervisor had assigned Tom to a job that he knew Tom disliked and wasn't qualified for. Tom was sure it stemmed from the supervisor's dislike for him. L. B. said he'd do some investigating. When he talked with the supervisor later, he discovered that it had been a bad situation indeed: one man was out sick, another transferred to a different department and Tom was the only one that could do the job. He had revolted when asked to do it because he didn't understand the whole picture. When L. B. explained it to him, Tom cooled down. L. B. had gotten the facts and set the picture straight. Later he smoothed things out with the supervisor.

L. B. has done similar digging on other occasions. Joyce, a billing clerk, once left a stack of invoices until it was past billing time while she went on a week's vacation. The department's first inclination was to get them out to the subscribers, but L. B. stopped any action in that direction until he did some checking. He discovered that a mistake had been made in drawing up the bills. Before she left, Joyce had alerted someone else to get the new invoices out.

Whether arbitrating or appraising, know the facts and be on sound footing.

## GETTING THE MOST OUT OF ANY IMPROVEMENT

If he improves a little, make hay out of it. My son has always been a finicky eater. He "doesn't like" many foods, probably because he has never tasted them. When we took him to a Chinese restaurant one night my wife had advised him, "Please try to like whatever is served." He did. I was amazed and hurriedly praised his taste in Chinese food.

When we praised his improved eating habits, he got even better. You'll find this also works with employees: pat them on the back for a little improvement and they'll knock themselves out improving further.

Any teacher will tell you the same thing: a student builds on improvement. Why not an employee?

One tempermental employee in Jake Parker's organization couldn't get along with people. It was almost impossible to deal with Nels. He had little understanding for people's requirements, eying only his own needs. If a man said that he wanted a job Tuesday, Nels told him how busy he was with all his problems. Jake felt he had to do something. He had a long talk with Nels, discussing his shortcomings in dealing with people and stressing his need to improve.

As a result, Nels started listening harder to others. He showed concern and really exhibited a completely different way of relating to people. This was no small accomplishment! Any improvement can be hard, but dealing with people can be especially difficult. Jake was quick to praise Nels when he deserved it. Nels was pleased with himself and kept improving. Finally Jake made him supervisor of a group. He's continued to do well and build on his improvement. Jake has another valuable supervisor rather than a slack worker. Be quick to see an improvement, no matter how small, and praise it.

## HOW TO UTILIZE SECONDHAND FEEDBACK
## FOR FIRST RATE RESULTS

Charlie Brinson was a newspaper advertising man who also acted as a press agent for improvement on one of his calls to a linen store.

He once told Elaine, the saleswoman, that more people would buy if she would stay out in the mid-section of the store. Previously she had spent much time in the back, only coming out when customers walked in. Her boss, Bob Hill, had mentioned this before but hadn't emphasized it. He was pleased to see Elaine paying attention to Charlie's advice, and said, "Let's fix a comfortable table and chairs in front of the spread display. If you can bring work out there to do, people will see activity and be more inclined to drop in." Both he and Elaine were pleased with Charlie's idea.

Did you ever hear compliments reverberate? It's terribly satisfying to hear someone pass along a compliment. A good thought will always make the rounds.

Hiram Jackson, vice president of a bank tried a different technique. He told a customer. The customer commented, "I know Wilma Lester well—we grew up together." Hiram responded "Wilma knows how to handle customers like an old pro." Later Wilma commented to Hi, "I appreciate what you told Mrs. Bennet. It made me feel good all over."

Firsthand compliments are fine; secondhand ones are, in many cases, even stronger.

## DISTINGUISHING BETWEEN JOB REQUIREMENTS AND PERSONAL REQUIREMENTS

You might have given a man enough information to get the job done but still his overall performance could slip. Does he know about your undefined requirements? Which characteristics in his overall behavior might handicap him?

When Sadie started working in the human factors department in a manufacturing company, her appearance was terrible. Carl Blake, the manager, had set down general standards for appearance, because while it didn't interfere with a job, but perhaps what was causing poor appearance might. He also felt poor appearance had a bad effect on morale.

When Carl talked with Sadie about it, he discovered that she had a problem at home. There wasn't much he could do about a drinking husband, but he listened and gave her honest sympathy. He then cautiously mentioned dress and makeup. "Sadie, you want your friends and fellow workers to see you at your best, even though you have a lot on your mind. Be sure to take a little time in the morning to highlight your best features. It'll boost your morale too," he said. Sadie agreed. When Sadie made the effort, her appearance did improve. Whether or not her home situation improved, she has taken on a more positive attitude toward her job environment.

Carl handled a similar situation of personal requirements within the plant. One of his best workers, Leonard Lanier, turned out one good job after another. His work was excellent. His desk, however, looked like a disaster area. Some might say that if someone turns out work as well as Leonard, he can do what he pleases with his desk. Carl, however, feared that it would be a bad example to Leonard's co-workers: he had preached and preached to his workers that he wants the whole area looking clean at night. How could he tell other workers that they must keep their desks clean, but that Leonard could make a mess since he did so much work. That wouldn't be fair. Carl sat down with Leonard and said, "Leonard, you are one of the best workers in the place, and the others look to you as an example. For that reason, you need to keep your desk in top condition. Set as good an example in the looks of this place as you do in your work." Leonard didn't really have that much trouble putting his desk in order once he decided to. Carl only had to get up his nerve and mention it.

Remember these suggestions for making the most of feedback:

—Give unfavorable feedback cautiously and in the right atmosphere in order to maintain motivation.
—Remove the sting from what you think is "constructive" criticism.
—Restrict your criticism to what will help him improve.
—Condition your people to expect feedback.
—Give an overall appraisal periodically.
—Listen in order to keep on the right track.
—Get him to help define the need for improvement.

Then get the most out of every little improvement that he makes.

# 10

## USING HONEST RECOGNITION TO GET AND SUSTAIN ACTION

Every man craves recognition—appreciation or importance. We've already learned that. You're not conning, cheating, or manipulating when you give it, but only satisfying a desire. Why can't we help a man fill that need while he is doing his work?

The average manager is slow to praise, but quick to criticize. You, the action-getting manager, should beat that average and know how to praise good work.

You should know

—How to give tangible and intangible recognition.
—How to use both positive and negative recognition.
—How to find favorable qualities in anyone.
—The use of group as well as individual recognition.

Start now by looking closer for praiseworthy qualities.

### HOW TO FIND FAVORABLE QUALITIES TO RECOGNIZE IN ANYONE OR ANY PERFORMANCE

One man's asset is another's liability, but even a man's asset can become a drawback in the wrong situation.

For example, one employee may have the ability to give orders to others. That's his asset. If he doesn't have any authority, or if he rubs people the wrong way in the process, it becomes a liability.

A person may be a good listener, actively encouraging others to talk. This could be a liability, however, if he uses that as a crutch and doesn't do his share in conversations or contribute to meetings.

Is a man "well organized" or is he just overly fussy about details?

Consider degree when determining what is an asset and what is a liability. There's little clearcut and indisputable difference. You've got to be a master at knowing your people. Only by close observation or constant checking on performance will you be able to spot qualities for recognition.

The obvious are quality, schedule and cost; add to that qualities, such as human relations ability, appearance and general behavior. What about housekeeping, safety, outside civic activities and political activities, community involvement, church work . . . the field is limitless. Praising an outside accomplishment might help to get him to improve his work. Utilize every angle.

There is a certain thrill in giving a man recognition. It's like the time a few years ago that my family went to pan for rubies. The first bucket of clay that I worked with yielded a ruby about as big as your little finger nail. I sat and panned until they had to come and unhitch my fingers from the pan so that we could go home. When you turn up a nugget of honest appreciation for a man, it makes you want to look more. Try it as a way of getting sustained results from your people.

## TAKING AN INTEREST IN INDIVIDUALS
## MAKES RECOGNITION EASY

It's absolutely necessary to observe your people closely. The quicker you cultivate a real interest in what makes a person tick, the easier it will be to make him feel appreciated.

Dave Hatcher, Chief Inspector on one of the crafts produced in an aircraft plant, showed how easy it is to translate an interest into a usable resource. When he decided he had the best team in the business and ran a survey to get more information about it, he discovered that he had 86 people with a total of 1,498 years of aircraft experience, 691 years of it on that particular plane; 24 different FAA licenses; 43

members of civic organizations; 12 past presidents of organizations; 21 members of church boards in some capacity. He published the information on the bulletin board and got an article written in the company paper. His men were impressed with their own credentials, as was the rest of the plant. Dave accomplished something else: he saw that each supervisor knew this vital information about his people and in the process created an interest in the individuals. The total result to Dave is high morale in his outfit. Anyone is pleased to be able to transfer into a division that shows this much interest in the individual man. Dave has more applicants than he can handle at a time when some of the other divisions are losing men right and left. The interest has led to recognition which has led to sustained high level of morale.

## HOW TO SATISFY A MAN'S DESIRE FOR IMPORTANCE AND GET CONTINUING RESULTS

Each of your men likes to be important to his group and his company. He likes to be recognized as an individual too. The key is in his day-to-day feeling about his job and how you see him performing it. We assume that individuals want to do good work. Give him benefit of the doubt and take every opportunity to confirm that you think he is important.

The industrial engineering department in a manufacturing company capitalized on the desire to be important: while advertising the department's accomplishments, it lets someone personally share the honors. A bulletin board was placed in a prominent place in the department with a poster reading: "The Industrial Engineering Department has helped solve 105 manufacturing problems this month. Thirty-two orientation sessions have been held for salaried and hourly workers. This would not have been successful without the assistance of Ann Johnson. She personally has scheduled and recorded the classes and attendance. She has maintained neat, accurate and efficient files. Thanks, Ann!"

Ann's so pleased with this salute to her importance that she looks like she founded the company. It could have been routine or mundane, but this recognition made it important to the company. Dan

Weaver, the industrial engineer, deserves credit himself for finding a way to raise individuals out of the ordinary.

## THE EXCEPTIONAL CASES WHERE NEGATIVE RECOGNITION IS EFFECTIVE

Does negative recognition get action? Under some circumstances it does. Use it carefully or avoid it in general, though. I'm talking about such awards as the "White Elephant."

If a group is doing miserably, you can sometimes give a booby prize that they must display for all to see (never single out individuals for such "awards," however). When another group does poorly, the award passes to them.

The Jaycees have done this in presenting a goat to the team that brings in the least new members. They have to keep the goat until the next month when someone else gets the dubious honor. It is all in fun and doesn't wound anyone's ego. That is the major point.

There is also the "Pig Pen" award given to the outfit with the poorest housekeeping performance. It reminds them to clean up the area and move the award along to another bunch. There might even be a plaque hung in front of the offending center.

George Alexander used this negative award in getting his office area cleaned up. He manages a tooling outfit of 75 to 80 people. They have 10 office areas that are all open space and create one big room. Housekeeping got sloppy and after many lectures on the subject, George asked his supervisors what should he do to get results. One of them suggested installing a "Pig Pen" award in the poorest kept area. It worked. After the first presentation the areas started looking better. The award was finally retired to a shelf with the prospects of being dragged out again if needed. The employees all seem anxious to keep their area from being labeled the "Pig Pen." This tactic can work, but use it cautiously and in good humor.

## MAKING VERBAL RECOGNITION PAY IN TANGIBLE RESULTS

Recognition doesn't have to be fancy to strike someone's fancy. It doesn't even have to be tangible. Just let him hear it. The only sound sweeter than praise is someone's own name. When you combine the two you really have a winner.

In the late 1960's there was a wave of "motivation" programs that swept the United States. The attempts at motivation involved some of the most ridiculous rewards imaginable. One company gave out green stamps to a person that worked a certain length of time without making errors. These stamps were redeemed in merchandise at the company's public relations office. It was soon learned that this type of activity made interesting public relations but only small inroads in motivation. Most managers with any sense went back to letting a man know when he does good work, even if it's just a pat on the back. You can still get great mileage out of a simple but honest word of praise.

Dan McDade manages an accounts receiving department. He watched Reg Poppel work several evenings until 6:00 on balancing accounts. This was Reg's own time and he was doing it because he wanted things right. Dan knew this from past experience with Reg, and stopped one afternoon to tell him so. "Reg, I don't want you to feel that you must stay every afternoon to try to catch up the accounts. But I do appreciate your attitude." "Aw, it isn't that much," he replied—but he was beaming. When Reg continued to show conscientiousness, Dan put him in a supervisory training program. Certainly his praise didn't do this! But Dan is a smart enough manager to give praise when it is due and ensure that the man knows that he is appreciated. The result will be a valuable supervisor who was encouraged to advance. The pat on the back may seem insignificant by itself, but it can produce management that cares about employees' work. Don't wait for some tangible means of showing appreciation—do it verbally at any opportunity.

## DECIDING WHAT WEIGHT YOU'LL GIVE MONEY AS A FORM OF ENCOURAGEMENT

While we're on the subject of money, let's look at the pros and cons of using it as an incentive. In a manufacturing company with a large and strong union, management has watched the effect of money as a motivator. It just doesn't do what it's supposed to do. Granted, a man must make a decent wage to have a roof over his head, food, clothing and a little luxury—but after he's got the basics, a little more money won't motivate him a little more. What will move him is:

—More appreciation.

—More recognition.

—A feeling of importance.

But what he says is:

I need more *money*." When he gets it he continues doing the same work at the same speed. He may even get older and staler.

Sales managers discovered long ago that a salesman won't work as hard for prize money as he will for trips, cars, and other glamorous awards he can flaunt. He'll even work just for the recognition of being Number 1. However, the use of money as a prize isn't considered the best incentive.

You need to decide just how much strength you'll place on money and other incentives as motivators. You may save a bundle and get better results in the process.

The outstanding engineer in the Static Test Engineering Department receives tickets to a baseball game. It isn't the size of the award but the fact that he has been singled out that's important. A rotating trophy is passed from employee to employee in a Master Scheduling outfit when a different person is saluted each month. At the year's end, one of them can keep it. It's a small investment with large results. These all single out a man for honor: the amount of the award is insignificant. You need to consider carefully how much you want to invest in the award. Don't fall into the old trap of thinking that more money will give more work. More *recognition* is the name of the game. That can come quite inexpensively.

## DECIDING WHETHER THE WHOLE GANG DESERVES RECOGNITION

Individuals love it, but so does the group. Maybe your recognition should embrace group activity, especially if one man or two couldn't do it and it took the whole group.

John Sherman, an inspection manager, accepted an award for top quality from the company's quality board. He accepted on behalf of his crew that worked on an assembly section. The award was given for improvement in reduction of discrepancies and "squawks" (minor discrepancies). John said the award covered a three-month period. He promptly turned it over to the people in his group. He did it in a ceremony commending Dick Wilson, supervisor, Earl Hester, lead man, and the other group members. "When mistakes are found, the supervisor and the lead men take time to tell the individuals how to fix it. They see that proper measures are taken so the same mistakes don't occur again." This is the way John explained it. He's smart enough to let his people look good and bask in reflected glory.

What about competition between groups? One company commended the best cost center each month by taking the members to lunch and giving them a complete plant tour. This type of recognition made the men more aware of what was going on all over the plant. It also made them pull harder to make their cost center look good. In plant maintenance, three groups were pitted against each other. The winning team got a chicken dinner from the others. Spirits were sky high: each man was out to see that his group won. They were judged on housekeeping, overtime, rework, absenteeism, safety, and several other factors. In the final week, Dan Brown, the manager, called them together for a few minutes to read off the averages and announce who would be buying the chicken. Amid cheering from one group and good-natured booing from the other two groups, a date was set and plans laid for the dinner. The groups are now anxiously looking forward to a rematch. Each is sure that they can outdo the others. Good spirit and good workmanship prevail. Maybe some good-natured competition would work in your place of business. If so, set some up on a formal basis. The least you can do is let the whole group know when it is meeting or beating the schedule or other basic criteria.

## HOW TO AVOID THE DANGERS OF INSINCERE RECOGNITION

In Dan Brown's example, the criteria was based on real standards. It's easy, however, to get sidetracked so that you are recognizing just for recognition's sake. I once saw a team of production men that was actually considering giving awards to men that read the company paper and could answer questions about it. That's contrived. Recognition ought to be according to regular job standards, unless it is a pat on the back for outside achievement. Remember that the real reason for recognition is to help a man fill a need. If it is contrived, he will know it, and you'll be worse off.

Your people know who deserves recognition. Unreal attention will turn them off. In a materiel department the manager, Paul Klien, got caught in just such a trap. He had seen some managers in other departments giving special recognition to their secretaries. (Vivian Motts had her picture on the board as Secretary of the Month in Customer Service. She deserved it.) Paul decided to follow suit. He called his secretary in and told her, "I appreciate your good work." Unfortunately, she is only average. He also broke a cardinal rule in not picking out anything specific to praise, but instead generalizing about her total performance. He put her picture on his department bulletin board with the notation, "Secretary of the Month." Two other girls in the department were annoyed. "Why her?" they asked. "She doesn't type well, keeps a sloppy desk and is late on occasion." Paul had laid an egg. He had to spend time soothing the others' feelings. He was only thinking of keeping in step with other managers. If you and I honestly think of the person we are dealing with, it will be a lot easier to make praise sincere.

## HOW TO TIME RECOGNITION FOR MAXIMUM EFFECT

Any time is right for praise. It is often helpful to give a man praise when things are not at their best and he needs a boost. For instance:

Mary Slagle had just worked on a long report. She had typed it over a couple of times before finally sending it to Property Accounting. In an hour, the supervisor called, told her about a mistake in the format, and then sent it back for her to redo. Mary is a very conscientious secretary who is right most of the time. However, the supervisor's words made her really despondent. Jim McPherson, group supervisor of the budget section, saw how depressed she was and asked, "What's the trouble?" Mary responded, "I can't do anything right and certainly can't please Larry Kitch. He sent the report back for me to do over." Jim said, "Mary, you know we all miss sometimes. You're fortunate in that you're right ninety-nine times out of a hundred. There aren't many secretaries that can beat that average. Just chalk it up to Larry's not being satisfied, hang in there and do it again." Mary smiled and went back to work. She was over the hurdle, but she really needed Jim's favorable comment to help get there.

Don't wait until the accomplishment has worn out to compliment him on it. Do it while the job is still in mind.

Another time to get maximum effect is when someone is really unsure of himself or his work. Floyd Hinson, a training manager, has a knack for giving a man feedback in a positive vein just when he needs it most. Fred Knowling conducted a course for chemists on their attitudes and self improvement plans. It was a sticky subject at best. Fred spent several weeks getting ready, had his material well planned and had maximum participation. Then it was all over. Fred had a feeling it went well, but no concrete proof. He wondered: "Should I change the direction for the next class? Should I give them more written work? Should I lecture less?" Floyd came in and congratulated him on a job well done. He had information from several of the students showing how they were already putting some of the material into effect. This praise gave Fred confidence to go full steam ahead with the next class.

Large companies schedule periodic appraisals every six to twelve months which forces the managers to make some comments, even if they are wrong. Too often appraisals only talk about needs for improvement, leaving recognition out. It's pretty hard for a company to force a manager to recognize employees. Why not keep a record of employee recognition? You may remind yourself in the process that one of your employees has gone too long without the praise that he needs.

## TELLING THE MAN'S BOSS IF HIS EMPLOYEE PERFORMS WELL

Another fine technique for passing along praise is through the man's boss or the chain of command. By inference, this compliments the boss for hiring and training such a man.

It happened casually, in a meeting: Bill Bement, manager of Foreign Sales, sat down opposite Clark Moreman, head of Government Sales. Bill got his attention and said, "Clark, that was an outstanding presentation that Clyde gave last week to General Clay. I sure appreciate your letting him do it. The General asked a lot of perceptive questions and established a good relationship with Clyde.

It should help us in the future." Clark was all smiles and said, "Thanks, Bill." Bill has done double duty. He has made Clark feel important and if Clark is worth two cents he'll pass the information along to Clyde, making everybody feel better.

It can be done formally, in a letter or note. One company uses IDC's (interdepartmental communiques) and commendations. These are both formal documents that do the trick.

Ernie Shuler wrote an IDC to a worker in another department for the man's boss to countersign. Ernie is the head of Structures Engineering and has been very active in the local chapter of Value Engineers. That chapter's annual convention took a fantastic amount of work. When Pat Wynn was asked to be general chairman, he pulled off the whole convention in fine style. Ernie's commendation of Pat was sent through company channels to Pat's personnel file. Everybody knew about it. Pat was thrilled at the attention, and Ernie was pleased to be a part of it.

Formally or informally, written or verbal, bringing the man's boss into the picture multiplies the effect.

## BUILDING RECOGNITION IN THE JOB ITSELF

Recogniton is a many-headed phenomenon. There are many ways to accomplish it without special effort on each occasion. It can be built into the job itself: parking place, special pass, office, desk, furniture, telephone book cover, secretary, or anything else special that goes with the job is worthwhile. Extras don't have to be tangible either. Let a man speak for you in meetings or represent you. It not only prepares him for harder tasks, it gives him real importance. Clark Moreman, Government Sales manager, knew that a briefing was coming up that half a dozen colonels would attend. It was an important meeting but Clark resisted the temptation to be there himself. Instead he called in Walt Johnston and asked, "Walt, how would you like to attend the briefing next week for Colonel Nelson and staff?" Walt's eyes lit up and he said, "Yes, I'd like it." Clark said, "I'm thinking of having you do the briefing." It was good exposure for Walt. He rehearsed for the briefing and had no trouble with it. It gave him a feeling of importance that increased his capabilities.

Clark, who is recognized as one of the company's best managers because of his ability to handle people, uses another technique that is really built into the job. Whenever a new man comes into his department or division, he turns him over to Jim Lewis for training. This part of Jim's job puts him in the limelight and shows that Clark has great confidence in him. It is a form of built-in recognition which illustrates Clark's concern for people.

A straw boss or lead man gets recognition from an assignment. One inspection manager has his men stamp their work with their own names testifying that it is correct; this makes them feel important. Let's look at some more of the ways that a man gets recognition in the line of duty.

## OFTEN OVERLOOKED MEANS OF GIVING RECOGNITION THAT ARE CLOSE AT HAND

These are the ones we just saw:

—Tangible awards.
—Verbal kudos.
—Letting a worker break in a new man.
—Asking him to give instructions to someone else.
—Letting him represent you at a meeting.
—Asking him to strawboss several people.
—Stamping his own work.

We should also mention these:

—Sending him to a training class.
—Letting him work with a minimum of direct supervision.
—Giving him a new assignment.
—Asking him for ideas.

## HOW TO USE YOUR COMPANY SYSTEMS TO MAKE THE MOST OUT OF RECOGNITION

A company newspaper, information sheet or house organ is a good place to spread the word.

A manufacturing company with 25,000 employees spotlights several workers each week. The article tells something about a man's background, kind of work and personal interests. It usually calls attention to his special skills. As with other group recognition, you have to be careful that it is sincere; otherwise, workers in his department will quickly see through the publicity.

The same company has bulletin boards in several hundred locations throughout its buildings. The personnel department selects a man every other week to feature on the boards with his picture and a few sentences about his accomplishments. Workers feel pleased that he is being congratulated and work toward meeting similar standards.

A Quality Improvement Board, composed of men from Engineering, Flight Line, Quality Assurance, Production, Tooling, Manufacturing Engineering, and Modification, meets weekly to work on problems of production or engineering. Hugh Caswell, manager of a Flight Line segment, had the idea of not only considering problems, but saluting good workmanship. They presented a special Top Quality Award each week to the cost center with the best record of inspection figures. The Board calls in managers, supervisors and lead men from the group to receive the award in front of the committee. Here's another idea of how a company system can be used to recognize good workmanship.

Even the customer can get into the act. The Air Force was the largest customer. Its contingent of men based in the plant decided to honor the group that they thought was turning out best quality. The Quality Control colonel used his inspections plus company records to select a production group periodically. The colonel calls a short meeting in the work area to present the award.

Use your housekeeping committee to recognize good housekeeping, your safety committee for safety, personnel department to recognize good attendance, etc. Every department can select its own top-performing individuals or groups that can be honored. Use your systems to furnish the leads and see that your people get their share of the limelight.

## USING THE PLUS FACTOR OF RECOGNITION WITHIN THE GROUP

It really pays off when a group recognizes its peers. Dan Brown's groups that had the chicken dinner thought of the scheme themselves and set out to make it work. One large department has a committee that helps select monthly award winners. Be careful, though: Wally Kramer, a purchasing manager, had a bad experience by letting others decide who got recognition. His committee selected a woman that they all liked, but who had given management trouble with absenteeism and lax office habits. Still, since her friends selected her, Wally was stuck with the choice of either turning down their selection or awarding a poor worker. If any employees participate in selecting honorees be sure that there is supervisory approval to steer clear of just such situations.

The workers may have a hand in looking at output and schedule performance. Dan's workers looked at legitimate figures.

## GETTING MORE THAN YOUR MONEY'S WORTH BY RECOGNIZING IN FRONT OF OTHERS

A person loves looking good in the eyes of his fellow workers. It's pleasing to think that they select him for recognition. Let them bask in their group limelight if possible. Announce awards and praise a man in front of the group.

Roy McKelvey supervises Production Control. Every Monday morning he meets with his whole department to discuss upcoming needs for the day and week. After they discuss any problems, Roy talks about accomplishments of the previous week. He said on one occasion, "I want to congratulate George O'Brien for the work he did on the parts inventory. He had the papers ready and the bins in order so that the inventory went smoothly. George, that was a good job." George was very pleased, and ready to sink his teeth into the next job. The other employees think more of Roy for saying that George did well.

There are literally hundreds of ways to recognize people. The vital issue is that you as an action-getting manager feel the need to do it and set up some system:

—Do it verbally or in writing.
—Make it tangible if you wish.
—Do it in front of his peers.
—Keep it sincere.
—Do it by using the ongoing company systems.

But above all else, *do it*. Use honest recognition and help sustain results.

# 11

## TURNING YOUR GROUP MEETING INTO AN ACTION-GETTING SESSION

Should you even have a meeting? That's got to be the first question. Some managers can't make a decision without consulting with several others. Maybe they're lonely—or just indecisive.

On an aircraft assembly line an inspector once stated to a supervisor, "That plane wheel needs air." The supervisor said, "Let me check it out with my manager." The manager went to the division manager and the division manager turned to his secretary and said, "Call Jim and Carl and Ted in here." He had to have a meeting to discuss putting air in the tires!

It is estimated that billions are spent each year on conducting meetings within organizations. The average executive spends half of his hours per week in some kind of meeting or conference. Do you *have* to have a meeting?

Is it to solve a problem for which there is no alternative?

Is it to disseminate information when there is no quicker way?

Is it absolutely necessary to pool opinions?

Will the men benefit from the attention resulting from staff or group meeting?

In a manufacturing firm, Facilities and Manufacturing Engineering holds a regular meeting each week to examine production problems:

—First-line supervisors and selected managers meet with manufacturing engineers.

—Complicated problems are spelled out and documented.
—They are then numbered and a person assigned responsibility for each.
—A report on the assignments is given at the next meeting.

The meetings have solved problems by bringing a better understanding to production and support personnel.

One outfit, a schedule control group, meets every day to examine contractors and the many items they furnish. They use a chart network that shows the up-to-the-minute status on all parts. This makes it easy to spot delays and take corrective action. This is another example of how a well-defined meeting can be used to get action.

Here are some suggestions to keep your action-getting session from dragging. They're going to be short and sweet—just like your meeting.

## HOW TO PLAN A MEETING

First be sure you know why you are having the meeting and what you expect to get out of it. After all, you are a man of action and there's no better place to exercise that attribute than in a meeting.

Define the purpose of the meeting:

"An RFQ (request for price quotation) on a new piece of electronic equipment."

"A problem solving meeting . . . 'We have a malfunctioning hose'."

"The reports are consistently late."

"We need a new adhesive on the gate section."

"A status meeting . . . to discuss budget, schedule, quality, or some other subject."

"Weekly staff meeting . . . to tell latest news and tie everything together."

There are dozens of legitimate reasons for holding a meeting.

Do you expect to leave the meeting with a decision, plan or change? What will be different? Will the people needed for a decision be there? Who's coming to the meeting? Where will you hold it? When will it be? How long will it last? What will be the style of participation?

If you have an efficient secretary, she can do much to facilitate plans for the meeting. Give her any of the information she needs.

Max Graham who manages an electrical pump assembly department is noted by his peers for having high morale in his outfit. One of the reasons is his staff meetings. His men know that at 8:00 AM every Friday they will be sitting in a meeting in his office. It's on everyone's calendar. One of his primary objectives in the meeting is increasing motivation. He lets each man talk about problems, concerns and/or accomplishments. He always has something to praise the group for and usually singles out individual accomplishments. The format of the meetings is simple, the purpose well defined, and they require little extra planning. Morale stays high because Max's people stay informed.

## BEING CHOOSEY ABOUT WHO ATTENDS YOUR MEETING

Please don't come to my meeting just because you don't have anything else to do.

With your own meetings, determine exactly who should attend, contribute the necessary information or need to hear the discussion. Who makes the decisions? Don't fool around with a flunkie: be sure the *right level* is represented in the meeting. Do you actually expect the decision to be made in the room? Is it within the power of the group in the room to take action, or should you invite someone else? Is more information necessary? Don't make an announcement if so.

Do send out a notice or tell the secretary who will be there. It'll help the man gage the general atmosphere ahead of time. It'll also help him arrive at his role.

Tim Cleveland, director of a Logistics Support Divison, uses this style:

| | |
|---|---|
| Subject: | Change of Shipping Dock Hours |
| Time: | 3:30 P.M. |
| Place: | Executive Conference Room |
| Attendees: | Supervisor of Loading |
| | Manager, Field Service |
| | Manager, Receiving |
| | Supervisor, Time Standards |
| | Personnel Representative |

Tim is noted as an efficient meeting holder: he's always sure that he invites the right people.

A man once walked into a meeting, took a seat and listened for almost 20 minutes before he picked up his note pad and headed back for the door. On the way out he was heard muttering, "I'm in the wrong meeting." He couldn't tell that he was in the wrong place. Be sure your attendees know who's to be there and why.

If you are going to run useful meetings, be selective about who comes.

## TELL THEM WHY THEY'RE COMING AND GET A BETTER FRAME OF MIND

Let the participants know why they are to be there and what is expected. They should have time to prepare to help the meeting succeed. Everybody loves a little bit of attention. If the man thinks he's going to look good in the meeting, he'll do his darndest. Also he thoroughly enjoys being told he is a needed authority: "Now, Tom, don't send someone else, because we need your personal opinion."

Tim told Doug Hires, the loading supervisor, "Doug, be sure to have your schedules with you. We need you to discuss the peak hours, number of men required, number of separate orders you are processing and any other statistics concerning man-hours on the dock."

Doug knows that when he shows up he is expected to help carry the ball. His information is vital to the meeting: he can't just forget to be there, have something else to do or respond, "I didn't know I was going to have to do that."

In a previous example when Max had asked his boss to attend the meeting, he wanted him to hear the discussion of a new plan that he would be a party to later. Even if the boss had strong feelings he should have known that he was only there to listen and get information.

If the man's organization will be affected down the line by a meeting, tell him so: "Jim, since your people will be the ones that will have to see that the decisions are put into effect, be sure that you are there to help get the kind of decision you want," or, "Jim, be sure and be there since you will have to inform your people what they will have to do."

Irv Foss, with 23 years of experience in managing production people, is noted as one of the keenest people-dealers in the business. He helped install a "Product Improvement Plan" in his production division. It was devised by higher-ups and was basically sound, but needed to be sold to Irv's men. The supervisors are the ones that have to do this.

Irv called a meeting of his supervisors. Previously he told them, "I want us to get together and pool our thinking on how to make the upcoming plan work. It is going to be rough to sell: we'll be blamed if it doesn't work. Do some thinking about it so we can devise a means to succeed." It was successful in the long run, because supervisors arrived at the meeting ready to do whatever necessary to put it across.

Follow Irv's example and charge your men to make a meeting work.

## TURNING THE ROOM INTO THE BEST BACKDROP FOR A SUCCESSFUL MEETING

Sometimes you have to be a producer, or at least a stage director. You are the boss of the meeting and need to start asserting yourself by getting the meeting place in the shape you want. The very best environment won't make a bad meeting good, but a poor environment can detract from an otherwise good meeting. So get it like you want it: don't be afraid to be particular about details.

How will you arrange the seating—classroom style? This can be terribly trite and boring. There are occasions when you may be showing a film or a slide presentation and need all eyes front. However, in most cases this can be accomplished from a conference table. The conference table puts everyone in view of everyone else. If you are going to let enthusiasm spread, it does so better when the seating arrangement is not disjointed as in a classroom.

Seats shouldn't be so comfortable that you doze off in them, but be sure they don't squeak, rock or fall apart. Nothing should detract from the meeting. If it is a fair size meeting and you want to try some psychology, just be one or two chairs short so that you have to send out for them. It'll make all the participants think "Everybody is knocking down the door to get in—glad I could be here." Do this advisedly. On the other hand, nothing is more demoralizing than to have an island of people surrounded by empty chairs.

Have plenty of light. Dim lights lead to dull wits. Keep them turned up. Even when you show slides or films, don't turn them completely out.

Perhaps the most succinct advice about equipment is use as little as possible and be sure it works well. If you can't work a slide projector or movie projector, have someone there who can. Be sure it is in working order. Walt Johnston of marketing checks out his equipment the day before, then gets it installed in the room as far ahead as practical and gives it a dry run in the room. He always gives a well conducted show.

Let's look at other ways to keep everybody happy and on their toes.

## EASY WAYS TO KEEP THE FOLKS AWAKE AND HAPPY

Pay attention to the people as well as the room. Their bodies will droop and their minds wander if you don't keep them interested. It's up to you to help them avoid boredom during the meeting. You should help them enjoy it.

If you have a meeting that is going to run over an hour, you'd do well to let them take a break.

Ask a man a question if he drifts away.

Get them to write down something.

Any kind of action will help.

Your enthusiasm, however, will be the real key to their staying awake and happy. Stand up yourself and talk a while if possible. Move around a little; it isn't necessary to run a meeting seated at the head of the table.

Call on someone at the other end of the table so attention and interest can move about.

Ask someone to keep the room temperature under control for you. Let one of the members be responsible for opening the window. It's better to keep it too cool than too hot.

David Shaife teaches a course in Human Relations. David gives his students a break in the middle of the two-hour class. He asks Jack Harris to keep track of the atmosphere. Since the students are allowed to smoke, it can get stuffy in a short time. Jack then gets up and opens the door or window. Dave's classes always hold the students' attention anyway, but just to be sure that the environment doesn't detract, he keeps it regulated.

In order to keep them awake and happy, stay enthusiastic, keep them involved, and maintain the right kind of physical environment.

## TIMING EVERY MOVE YOU MAKE FOR A BETTER PAY-OFF

Part of your plan is knowing when to start, when to stop and how to be great in between.

Let's start with starting. It's like diving into cold water: it takes a little courage, and you have to keep on swimming once you get in. It is easy to delay the opening with "Maybe Max will be here in a few minutes," "Oh, I hate to start with two people missing," "Jane said she would be here for sure." Don't wait on Max, Jane or anybody else. There's no telling what they've decided to do instead. Start on time.

Richard Tanner, a marketing supervisor, dramatized his feelings about getting to a meeting on time. In a series of marketing meetings that he conducted, he locked the door at the starting time, and made all late-comers knock to get in. After the first day, everyone was there on time. The other attendees appreciated his respect for their time.

Sandy Martin, a Finance manager, was even more blunt. He looked up as two men straggled in twenty minutes late to his budget meeting. Calmly he asked, "Did you come early for tomorrow's meeting?" Everyone chuckled. Sandy knew the men could take it without serious offense. However, they all got the point that he expected people to get there on time.

Don't wait for anyone unless he is the boss and you're absolutely sure he'll fire you. Even then, can you start with something that he can catch up with?

If a man on the program is late, can you start with someone else and fit him in later? You owe something to the attendees. Why make them pay for someone else's lack of punctuality?

The same applies to ending on time. You are the only one responsible for this. The best time to stop a meeting that was to run for an hour is at the end of the hour. Stop sooner if you've covered everything. I've conducted meetings that were completed in one-half hour and told the participants, "I guess that's it," and watched shock creep across their faces. Most people are used to running over into other meeting time.

Keep an eye on the deadline and summarize in time to make it. Put your watch on the table in front of you if necessary. Those with other meetings to attend will be grateful.

The middle of the meeting takes considerable planning. The other sections of this chapter will help you do this. Basically, define the purpose and goals of the meeting; then get the necessary information before the group so that the objective can be accomplished on time. That includes getting enough participation from the right people and controlling the whole show.

In selling, every move is aimed to closing the sale. In running a meeting, every move is aimed to meeting the avowed objective on time.

## SELLING THE BENEFITS OF THE MEETING
## TO A PARTICULAR GROUP OR INDIVIDUAL

Because managers attend so many meetings they tend to take them for granted. Why should they bother to go when they have other more important things to do? If you want them at your meeting let them know why it is important for them to be there. If you need their input, let them know. Putting their names on the notice you send out helps alert them and everyone else.

Bart Cramer had to conduct cash conservation meetings in one of the production company's branch plants. The local manager, Ed Crates, wasn't anxious to participate at all. He wished Bart would stay at home and mind his own business. However, the president had said do it, so he had to. The preliminary meeting that he held worked well. When time came to write up the meeting notes Bart decided to do some more selling. He began the minutes by stating: "Congratulations on creating a cost-conscious team. Sessions held October 5 after the original meeting show that the necessity for cash conservation has been realized. Savings indicate long-range rather than short-range results. Here in the supervisors' own words are the results so far: _____." Here he listed some of the results. It was a motivating paper and helped to spur Ed to continue the work. Bart took time to sell benefits to a key man.

During the meeting, it is well worth while to stop periodically and define our goals and accomplishments. Keep reminding the group why it's all necessary: "We're trying to get the solution now;" "We're after information on the causes of this problem and we'll work on the solution later;" "We're trying to get the best means of setting up the schedule."

In Irv Foss's meeting to sell the Product Improvement Plan, Irv stopped many times to challenge the supervisors. "Dale, are you sure you know how you are going to use this in the Heavy Equipment Section?" "Mark, how do you intend to get your people to feel that they have a stake in making this plan work?" He was then sure that his men not only understood the plan, but were committed to making it work. He was selling the benefits of this particular meeting indirectly as he sold the benefits of the action planned.

Time is valuable, to say the least—and meetings are really time consuming. Use your time well and make your attendees know that it was worthwhile.

## KEEPING CONTROL SO THAT YOU CAN ACCOMPLISH YOUR OBJECTIVE

To get the most out of a meeting, you often have to place time limits on compulsive talkers as well as encourage some to participate in discussions. Some people just won't shut up and let someone else talk. Try saying: "Jake, we know you really feel strongly about that, but let's hear from someone else." Don't give him the floor. If worse comes to worse, have a short break and tell him he needs to let someone else talk. If everything else fails, just tell him he's taking too much time.

Don't let side conversations break out. You can't run two meetings at once. Tell them, "Let's have just one meeting at a time." Be sure you don't talk to *your* neighbor.

Once I was conducting an orientation for a visiting Air Force group. About 50 people were in the room and we were well under way. Suddenly a major came in, climbed across six people to get to a seat and started talking to his neighbor. I just stopped and watched him. Soon everyone else in the room was watching him. When he saw this he shut up, sat up, and paid attention. It takes courage to maintain silence, but the crowd will appreciate your getting order.

If someone is speaking too softly, ask if the people in the back or on the other end of the table can hear him. If not, ask him to speak a little louder.

If you see that someone's not making himself clear, ask him to explain again. Remember that you're in control. If people don't get what they should from the meeting, you are to blame.

Handing out printed material at a meeting can be a problem. If you don't control it, it can detract from your meeting. I've seen scores of otherwise capable managers walk into the room, hand out notes and then start talking. A man can't read and at the same time listen to you—and he sure can't hold that piece of paper in front of him and not read it. If you hand out notes, allow time to read them. You might even read it with them. Don't try to talk while they are reading.

The leader—that's you—must control the meeting. Do whatever is necessary to maintain order, clarity and participation. You'll get applause for running a good show.

## GETTING ON THE SAME WAVELENGTH WITH YOUR GROUP

This might mean saying, "I know no one wants to make the decision on the management development names. But it is stupid for us to let the decision be carried up the line because we are afraid to act. Let's do it." This was the approach used by Dave Hatcher in the Quality Assurance organization after the group of managers had fussed and fumed about what they couldn't do. Dave put it on a sensible plane and got everyone on the same wavelength. He is a leveler who consistently does this.

Start off with a statement of *why* the meeting is being held: "We are going to *discuss* the changing of hours on the loading dock;"

"We are going to *change* the hours on the loading dock;" "We are going to *listen* to the information on loading dock hours;" "We need to look at ways of improving safety in the plant;" or "Finance states that our cash flow is seriously in danger. We must *determine* ways to conserve cash."

Tell participants why each was asked to attend, if it is appropriate.

"John, you have the information on the hours."

"Sam, you are directly affected by the timing."

"Buck, you are going to have to clear the time with Personnel."

Make any other comments that seem appropriate. This kind of statement tells a man why he's there and what is expected from him.

You can't beat clarifying the meeting purpose and subject as a way to get everyone on the same wavelength at the start.

State what the time limits are. "We'll finish by 10:00." "We are going to take an hour and a half to do it."

Your beginning with a regularly scheduled group meeting is as simple as "Good Morning. Let's see how we did last week and what we need to pay particular attention to this coming week."

You might periodically summarize information: "So far we have looked at the hours, the load, and the schedule; now let's look at personnel." Keep putting it all together for the participants. Recapitulate for those that don't seem to know what's happening and see that they understand. You can keep this momentum going right through to a unified conclusion.

## DRAWING THAT FINE LINE BETWEEN
## DISCUSSION AND APPROPRIATE DISCUSSION

Something doesn't necessarily have to be off the subject to be unnecessary to the meeting. The discussion can be terribly interesting and still not be directed toward the main purpose. You may have to move in and cut it short, saying "Let's look again at our purpose." That's what you're there for.

Wayne Williams, Production Control Supervisor, chairs a warranty committee that has to coordinate the thinking of six or eight major departments in arriving at action on some unsatisfactory item. In one meeting the subject was a pin-down latch in the cargo department. The men were examining the whole thing looking for a way to keep from cutting a finger when the loading crewman reaches back behind a bundle to latch down the cargo. One enthusiastic participant started talking about how cargo that was delivered to Ecuador last week was loaded in maximum time. The question arose in Wayne's mind whether this discussion was going to help them with their decision, particularly when the fellow grew eloquent in describing the trip. Finally Wayne said, "Charlie, let's get back to looking at the latch itself." They then proceeded to solve the requirement and get out of the meeting on time. Wayne had to listen, analyze and act.

A meeting of merchants in a shopping center was called to work on getting a stop light. One of the members brought up the need to start investigating decorative lights for Christmas. It was the right subject and group, but the wrong time to discuss it. The leader wisely said, "Let's wait till our next meeting when we can give it full treatment."

Another session approved an advertising campaign. The advertising committee normally provides a complete plan that the group more or less rubber stamps unless it is something very inappropriate. But this time one of the men was curious about advertising rates: "How much per inch?" In a short time the whole group was immeshed in figuring cost and space. Ray Thrasher, the leader and a smart manager, saw what was happening and called a halt. "We have a committee to do this. Let's let them do it on the outside." Ray made the right move and let the managers get into some other items that did need to be resolved by them.

Limit your actions to what concerns your avowed meeting purpose. This adds to your success as a meeting chairman.

## HOW TO GET JUST THE RIGHT AMOUNT OF PARTICIPATION AND NO MORE

Ask questions, but make them brief.

Make assignments, but speed them up.

Get opinions, but condense them.

Don't go around the room and ask each man in turn what he thinks, like calling the role. Do see that each one has his share of attention. It is possible to sit through a meeting and feel that no one knew or cared that you were there.

Encourage questions from the members if appropriate, but then know how to handle them. Some meetings lend themselves to questions and answers; others don't. You may have to set the pace. If you ask for questions, allow time for answers. Avoid saying, "Well, if that's all of the questions, I guess that concludes the meeting." Save one strong point on which to end. Cut off the questions just before the last one is asked. Some people can waste valuable time asking too many questions. You may have to ignore them or turn them off.

The hardest task for the meeting runner is to shut up the man who is going great guns about his favorite subject. This must be done. It's possible for him to be on a completely pertinent subject and still be hogging the floor. Can you get another participant to give the same input and let the other cool down for a while? You might try: "Jim, you're really wound up on that subject, could we hear from someone else for a while?" No matter how smart he is, the rest of the group could get tired of him, so don't let him take over—otherwise, why bring the other authorities in the first place.

A meeting that is well maintained has a good after-effect. Charlie Bostick, a flight line director, holds a regular meeting with all of the organizations that have representatives at the flight line of an aircraft plant. He makes sure that one of his subordinates alerts each person as to which items will be on the agenda and what is expected of them. But most important, Charlie sees that it happens—that the desired participation comes to pass. He's likely to say, "Dale, give us your new parking plan or the directions for traffic flow." Or, "Stacy, tell us how you have planned the safety campaign out on the line." He makes it move by getting what's needed to fill the agenda.

### GETTING THE RIGHT INFORMATION FROM THE RIGHT PEOPLE MAKES THE MEETING

Many of your smartest men are the shyest in meetings and would be happy to let someone else do all of the talking. Even if a man is an authority on a particular subject, you've often got to draw him out with questions like, "Steve, how do you see this change affecting Master Scheduling?" or "What is the situation in Programming?"

Dave Walgren has a knack for getting the right information. He's superintendent in a tooling department and much like Charlie Bostick, can draw the best from participants. A meeting with design engineers, inspectors, production supervisors and schedulers was going well when the point came for someone to discuss the design features in one of the large fixtures that was giving production trouble. The design allowed people to steal parts from the main fixture for use on others, causing imperfection in the final product. Each attendee had contributed what he could. Webb Tate, an authority in designing large fixtures, almost let the meeting end without opening his mouth. He had information that the group needed, so Dave chided, "Webb, we need your say. What should be done?" With that he started the flow that got the desired information for the group. Later the head of manufacturing thanked Dave for solving the problem. Dave didn't solve it, but he was smart enough to get the information from someone who could.

When you know who has information you need, don't be afraid to pry. You invited certain people because of their expertise—don't let them leave without getting it before the group.

Next best thing to knowing something is knowing someone else who does and how to tap his knowledge for your use.

## HOW TO USE THE MINUTES OF A MEETING
## TO FURTHER THE CAUSE

The minutes represent one of your handiest tools, or one of the most boring. They should:

Inform.

Get action.

Go on record.

It all depends on how you write and use them. For example, if you include a notation that "the public relations department will contact the Marysville paper and reserve space," follow it up with a parenthetical notation (Attention: Jay Wilkins) or (Action: Jay Wilkins). Circulate the minutes to all concerned persons. It saves a lot of correspondence and perhaps further meetings as well.

Another excellent way to get action is to show a distribution list at the bottom of the minutes. This means if an action item is listed for

Jay Wilkins and a copy goes to Claude Thomas, his boss, then Jay is even more likely to be put into action. It's very effective.

People are more likely to take action if you tell everyone that they are committed to it.

A distribution list also saves a man from calling and saying, "Did you know they decided in the last Quality Control meeting to eliminate the data processing report?" He can see that the man concerned got a copy of the report.

Put things to be recorded in a file. Check back later to see that they're done—certainly before the next meeting—so that any necessary action or reporting can be done at the meeting.

Dick Weston acted as secretary at the Quality Improvement Board Meeting. His notes were terrible: unoriginal, long-winded and certainly not action oriented. When Dick was away for several months, Bill Lasseter filled in. The chairman and committeemen, as well as all recipients of the minutes, saw a vast improvement. Bill followed this format:

### NOTES ON QUALITY IMPROVEMENT BOARD MEETING
March 18, 19—

The regular weekly meeting was held at 1:00 PM in Conference Room B with these attendees:

B. A. Alexander, Dept. 10-01 chairman

| | |
|---|---|
| Norman Apple 98-03 | Henry Marshall 57-01 |
| Robert Butts 73-44 | L. C. Meyers 41-01 |
| Charlie Cooke 38-03 | Nick Prather 46-02 |
| Ernest Erskin 57-01 | Capt. Simmons Air Force |
| D. P. Wheeless 94-01 | R. C. Little 57-01 |

*Top Quality Award* was presented to the Forward Wing Section, 89-01. John Sherman, manager, Tim Conners, supervisor, and John Browne, lead man, accepted. They deserve congratuations for producing two sections on time without discrepancies.

*P. D. Tags.* L. C. Jackson stated that the number is up to 178 with 15 old ones not received in B-5 ramp area (Attention: Ned Fricks.).

(Bill recorded all major areas discussed, action needed and persons responsible.)

These minutes inform, permit action to be taken, and act as a permanent record for management.

Bill also compiles a copy list of people other than attendees who should receive copies.

Unfortunately for Dick, but fortunately for Bill, when Dick came back the chairman stated that he thought they would just continue with Bill since he had the situation under such good control. His organized action-getting minutes paid off. Use your minutes to get the most from your meeting.

When you start to write the minutes, clarify what happened. Don't just record every action and comment. Relate them to the purpose of the meeting to paint a clear picture for the recipient. Simplify too —some managers like to use a telegraphic style where incomplete sentences state the action in a hurry. The occasion, company and meeting purpose will determine style.

An example: "Recommended that checks be countersigned. Approved by all. Finance to do it. Budget recommendations: report each Wednesday; voted to go into effect next Wednesday, June 3."

Even if you don't use telegraphic language, keep things simple and summarize as much as possible. If you have the confidence of the group you may even editorialize a little—but be careful here.

Example: "The group was enthusiastic about moving closing hour from 6:00 to 4:30." "Most of the members refused to be a party to any lawsuit. Maybe we should get out of the association completely."

Keep in mind that you are still the leader, even on paper. Use a strong hand to control the minutes, just as you would the meeting. See that every word and statement strengthens your cause.

## WHAT TO DO AFTER THE CROWD LEAVES
## TO BE SURE THAT YOU DO GET ACTION

You still have a job to do after the crowd leaves. You then have to figure out who gets a copy and how strict to make the action requirements. I never settle for passive notations about what was accomplished. The writing of the minutes is very important. The language used should spur activity. Instead of saying "The committee decided that public relations should contact the paper," say "Public relations will contact the paper and negotiate." Use the action requirement mentioned earlier: (Action: Jay Wilkins).

You might even need to put in a telephone call to clarify any details, get action started or see that action is on track before the next meeting.

Remember the importance of wording the minutes right and setting up a follow-up system. You could have the complete key to final results in your hands either on paper or in the way you set up follow-up.

Mark on your calendar anything that needs following up at a certain time. File a copy in your day-to-day file so that it's there on the day an action should be completed.

If you feel that a person needs more lead time to take action, don't wait until he can receive the minutes—call him and get him started. If he needs more information than the minutes contain or special treatment, provide it for him.

Here's how Mike Arkoff handled one recalcitrant participant after a meeting. Mike, the head of scheduling, had called the meeting to get a better system of stock flow. He knew Joe wasn't happy but could not spend more time with him in the meeting, so he went to see him the minute the meeting was over, saying, "Joe, I know you will be concerned that your group is asked to keep the records on stock exchanges. I realized in the meeting that you were upset about it. I'm not sure that the Stock Control group as it is now organized can do it, and we can't afford to take the chance at the moment. But your people can do it. Let's give it a whirl and if you are still concerned, we will try to make a change."

Perhaps the best test is reviewing in your own mind the progress of the meeting and the minutes. Can there be results as it now stands? If not, take whatever action necessary to bring them about.

## CAPITALIZING ON YOUR OWN ABILITIES IN RUNNING MEETINGS

The best advice that you as a manager can get in using your abilities to run meetings is: Be yourself. There's no reason that a meeting should change a warm person into a cool formal chairman.

Your manner, style and personality will suffice to keep the meeting on a natural plane. We are often inclined to change personalities and leave out everything that sells us. It almost happened to my wife:

Mary asked me for some help in preparing a speech of introduction for a school president. She said, "He's one of the warmest, most down to earth, enjoyable people that I have ever met. It was a pleasure to go with him around the school as he spoke to the pupils and see the mischief in their eyes as they spoke to him. He told stories about the school. With a twinkle in his eyes, he said that he worried about the path between the boys' and girls' dorms until he discovered one day that the path had been made by plumbers and other workers moving between the two buildings."

"He also told about a boy and a girl getting walkie-talkies for Christmas. They communicated between the dormitories. He dropped subtle hints that he knew what was going on, and finally he had to tell them. He had a walkie-talkie too. He had been tuned in and didn't want to interfere with their conversations."

Mary was to introduce him to a group that included school teachers, principals and superintendents. These were the facts she wanted to cover:

—The man was born in Dallas, Ga.
—He married a woman from Manchester.
—He attended school in West Georgia.
—He got a masters degree from the University of Georgia in Agricultural Science.
—He worked on a doctor's degree and was finally chosen for this job.

She said, "This is the kind of thing that I need to say about him," and began to quote the facts.

"You're going to miss the boat," I told her, "if you don't inject some of the gentleman's warmth and feeling. The audience, after all, is looking to you for its first impression of the speaker. They don't want you to make his speech for him, but you're supposed to help set the pace. You should be able to use the same warmth that you told me about."

She replied, "Well, that's not like me."

"It was like you while you were sitting and talking with me. Why isn't it like you if you're talking to them?"

She finally agreed that maybe I had a point, and planned a very simple introduction about how she was impressed by the speaker's warmth and humor on the trip to Tallulah Falls, using a few examples of his down-to-earth qualities. With a few other facts, she presented him to the audience. All this did not take much over a minute.

The result was warm, unpretentious and appropriate because she said what she felt, in her own style.

Your style will work beautifully. Do your best with it.

Once again, to keep your meeting from being a drag:

Plan it . . . plan it . . . plan it.

Get the right people, tell them why they're there, and get the right information from them while they're there.

Control the meeting; keep it on track and on time.

After the meeting is over, write, phone or visit to see that what ought to be done is done. Use the minutes to get results.

## GOOD LUCK

You've spent time examining ways to get action:

—Breaking down assignments for simplicity,
—Defining standards,
—Building in checkpoints for follow-up,
—Giving recognition and correction,
—Giving help for necessary improvements.

You've looked at ways to sell yourself in speaking to your group.

As you know by now, action-getting is a state of mind. You've got to expect action, demand action and be willing to give action yourself.

You've got to know what action is. Add determination or persistence to it, and you're on the way. Don't let anyone sidetrack your determination to get action and manage successfully!